DOG CULTURE

WRITERS ON THE
CHARACTER OF CANINES

Edited by Ken Foster

The Lyons Press
Guilford, CT
An imprint of The Globe Pequot Press

Contents

INTRODUCTION

Ken Foster

Last spring I found myself at an elegant catered cocktail party. I had been out of town for most of the previous year, so there was a lot of catching up to do among the other guests, some of whom had no idea that I'd ever left or returned. One of these guests, a poet whom I knew only from having been at many of these types of things before, listened patiently as I countered her truly exciting news of a book deal with my own news: I had adopted a dog, and no longer had any interest in anything else. I say she was patient because I am sure I went on far longer than would be interesting even to someone who liked dogs at all. But what she said next revealed that she was of that other type of person.

"You don't hug and kiss him, do you?" she asked. She seemed confident that my response would be in the appropriate, reassuring negative.

"Oh, all the time!" I said, and the poet retreated into the crowd to find someone, anyone, to talk with.

A few months earlier I would have been on her side. Dogs, and their people, had little interest to me, and I certainly couldn't imagine what it was that they found so wonderful, so charming, so fascinating and admirable about their beasts. But there they were, wherever you went, clogging sidewalks, taking over parks, building separate rooms and homes, checking the Internet for resorts that would welcome them on vacation. But I'd been converted by a dog in Costa Rica, by strays in Havana, and when I returned to my empty apartment in empty Manhattan, it was clear to me that there was something I'd been missing all this time: a dog.

Once I found him, he introduced me to a whole new crowd. One of the great things about dogs is that they are blind to occupation and politics, so I ended up meeting new people whom I might never have otherwise known: doctors, lawyers, printers, chefs. Having a dog meant spending hours every day outside, on the street, in the park. It forced me to reenter society, albeit a subculture I'd never been a part of before. He also reintroduced me to friends I'd lost touch with, all of whom had recently, even reluctantly, acquired a dog.

Dogs, and their people, seemed better, somehow more whole and profound than either creature on its own. There were qualities you could assume about people with dogs, particularly if the dog in question was a scrappy mutt whom someone (a previous owner) had left tied out on the street alone. Dog people were generous, caring, eccentric. How else to explain the proliferation of doggie day-care centers and gourmet kibble made with human-grade ingredients? Do I even get to eat that well? My dog certainly does, chowing down on Wellness Chicken Super 5 with hormone-free chicken, blueberries, sweet potatoes, peas, brown rice, et cetera. Meanwhile, I'm scraping together a ketchup sandwich on stale bread.

Dog people can also be completely nuts. Dangerous, desperate, cruel. But even people who keep dogs for the purpose of fighting them have a bond with the animal that they don't share with another human. Harder to explain are the Wall Street traders who frequent the park, turning beet red and threatening to kill anyone who doesn't appreciate their "delicate" chow, whom they perversely refer to as "my girl."

Who but a dog would be gracious enough to stick with someone like that?

In assembling this collection, I asked a variety of people to write about aspects of the dog world, but to avoid writing about their own dog. The last thing I wanted was a collection of otherwise intelligent people droning on and on about how their dog was different, more special than all the rest. And yet it quickly became apparent that this was an impossible assignment. What better example of disobedience or love is there, what specimen has been more intimately studied than your own dog? And so the personal details pop up here and there, but, like the best writing on anything, each of these essays is both about a specific dog, and about all dogs, and, most important of all, about something bigger and more essential than just dogs themselves. Life, and how we choose to live it.

Given my own experience, it shouldn't be surprising that so many of these writers mention their initial ambivalence toward their dog. In "What Coco Ate," René Steinke describes her initial revulsion at her boyfriend's dog and, more particularly, his shameful gluttony. Brent Hoff is similarly reticent when his girlfriend, after cruising dog rescue sites as if they were "Internet porn," comes home with a baby pit bull who defies the racial (breed) profiling that preceded him. Dogs were forbidden in the Chassidic community in which Pearl Abraham was raised, but that didn't stop her from eventually getting a dog of her own, demon or not.

Much as we'd like to think otherwise, dogs don't charm everyone, and sometimes the ire they inspire is well deserved. I worried that I wouldn't find someone willing to go on the record as a dog hater, but Elissa Schappell gallantly agreed to fill the bill. Her rant against every drooling, expectant, mooching mutt is as hilarious as it is absolutely wrong. And in his contribution, Chris Offutt describes the Kentucky dog of his childhood, locked out of the house, injured with buck-shot, but still deeply loved.

If we are talking about dog culture, then we must talk about dog fashion; T Cooper examines dogs as accessories and accessories for dogs, and reveals her own stage-dog-mom ambitions for her miniature pinscher. In talking about the acquisition of her first and second dogs, Hillary Rosner explains how her city dogs allow her to hold on to her fantasy of escaping into the wilderness. For Terese Svoboda, raising two dogs means struggling with the fear that her dog daughters will age fast enough to become her nagging mother in "Girl Dog Mom." And in "The Dog Guilt Trip," Nicholas Dawidoff explains that he is, unmistakably, responsible for the obnoxious behavior of his labradoodle.

Chuck Palahniuk and Annie Bruno both round out the collection with more serious pieces, Chuck portraying the working life of a rescue dog through the eyes of his master and her album of photos. Annie details the final days of her epileptic dog, and the strange bond we form with animals in spite of the certainty that we will outlive them.

My own essay, "How to Be Alone," began with my observations of the dogs in Costa Rica, and at the urging of friends turned slowly toward a study of my own dog's obsessively strong pack mentality.

Today, as I print out these pages, Brando first rests his head on top of the printer, then slides his enormous snout into the paper tray, where the essays unfurl, page by page, against his nose. Is it the vibration that he finds comforting, or is he just doing his best (which is generally very good) to come between me and whatever might pull my attention away from him? The "dog freaks" I once belittled might suggest that he knows something about what this project is and the role he plays in it. And in spite of myself, I'd like to believe them.

Ken Foster
March 2002

WHAT COCO ATE

René Steinke

I didn't like that wet fur and Purina smell, I didn't want claws ripping my stockings or bits of fur stuck in the rugs, and I had a hard enough time feeding myself, much less feeding another creature. I was a jogger, and dogs had chased me so often that if I saw or even heard one, I'd turn and run in the other direction. I didn't really get why people would want to have a dog—it seemed like a hobby for people who didn't know what else to do with their time.

In my late twenties, I moved to New York City, and I began to date Craig, and Craig had a dog, Coco. On one of our early dates, we had to go back to his apartment after the movie to walk the dog before dinner. I was wearing high platform sandals, and I stumbled back when Coco jumped on me with his paws on my dress, barking into my bosom. Annoyed and startled, I tried to look cool. Craig was smiling widely. "Coco, get down," he said, sounding more amused than firm. Coco was a nine-year-old mutt, part husky, part shepherd, part golden retriever, a dog Craig had adopted from the pound. His fur, various shades of brown and black, was thick and sprinkled over the wood floors of the apartment like tiny scratches. He panted and drooled, and licked Craig on the face. "He likes you," Craig said, but I was not charmed.

Craig was the editor of a magazine, worked long hours, and frequently went out at night to hear music. Our dates were flirty, exhilarating, the kind when there's always more to say than you can, the time passing quickly until the disappointing moment when Craig had to go home to walk the dog. Grudgingly, I realized that if I wanted to continue to date Craig, I would also have to date his dog.

It didn't help that Coco had once been shared with Craig's ex-wife, who still stopped by now and then to pet and fawn over her ex-pet. It was obvious Coco preferred her to me. And to make matters worse, Coco was not well trained, and I was used to well-trained dogs, at least if they were in the house.

I was brought up a Protestant, and despite the four children and pets, our home was basically restrained and neat. We did our homework before dinner, which was at five-thirty, and we weren't allowed to have soda, white bread, candy, or junk food. Our vegetables were boiled, served without butter. We cleaned our rooms and did the dishes.

A Protestant is taught by rote, work before pleasure, work before pleasure. And dog trainers also invoke a version of this wisdom: Give your dog a treat after he obeys a command; withhold the treat if the dog disobeys the command. Vicki Hearne, the poet and animal trainer, argued that dogs want to work and to learn, that they will seek to accomplish tasks if they are worth accomplishing and meaningfully rewarded.

But Coco had no work, he had only his pleasures, or his pleasures were his work, depending on one's perspective. And most of his pleasures involved various things he put into his mouth. In the beginning, I found his voraciousness shocking. Once Craig and I came home from a date to find the remnants of a used tampon torn up on the floor, and another time, we found a used condom licked clean and left for us on the bed. I did not warm to this behavior, and often felt as if Coco were looking for new ways to disgust me. He devoured bandages coated with pus and blood. He sucked on dirty tissues. He drank out of the toilet bowl.

"How can you let him do that?" I'd say to Craig.

"You try stopping him," he said.

Coco ate: eggshells, cellophane, Band-Aids. Cough drops, coffee grounds, the shit of certain large dogs, chicken bones, large insects, lip balm, Cheez Doodles, torn-out, water-stained pages of a phone book, toothpaste, corn on the cob.

There were two things that defined Coco: his appetite and his devotion to Craig. He slept in Craig's bed, and usually gazed at him while he fell asleep; he followed him around the apartment; he drooped listlessly on the couch when Craig was away and whimpered when he saw a suitcase. Craig understood it as gratitude to him for having saved Coco's life.

Coco's papers said that he'd first belonged to two young males, but one was deceased, and Craig theorized that it might have been a gay couple, one of whom had died from AIDS. He was sure that only a traumatic force of circumstance would make someone give up such a great dog. The story of their meeting went like this: Craig and his ex-wife walked into the pound, where all the other dogs barked and snarled in their cages, while two-year-old Coco sat, quietly wagging his tail, amiably cocking his head, as if to say, "Pick me! Pick me!" It might have been the only time in his life Coco restrained himself.

Coco was only medium sized, not large, but he was a barker, and he'd bark right up your leg as if considering whether or not he would bite it when he ran out of things to say. "He thinks you want to eat his food," Craig would say to our wary guests. He was talking about the little bowl of pellets that sat in the narrow hallway near the front door. Coco may have preferred to lick Craig's plate or to scavenge a bone from the street, but he did love his pellets, too. He had a ritual of pawing a few of them out of the food bowl and dancing with them before he ate them. He guarded that food bowl as if it were the last of his provisions, barking at everyone who came through the door, children, repairmen, friends he'd scented a dozen times before. He should have been chasing and barking at the mice, which actually were eating his food, but he was not a mouser and didn't even see them. The mice took Coco's little pellets and gnawed on them behind the bookcase, in the closet inside a pair of shoes, under the bed. We'd find the brown crumbs clumped together with bits of Coco's shed fur. The irony was that what Coco so intently guarded was being spirited away from him, little by little. But there was a big difference between the mice's appetite and his. Coco's appetite was never secret.

At first, Craig's dog and I only tolerated one another. Finally, he stopped barking at me every time I passed his food bowl and every time I lunged to kiss Craig (protecting him from me). And when Craig and I began to live together, though Coco's habits still made me squeamish, I cleaned up after him and even took up half of the dog-walking responsibilities, appalled at the newspaper-under-the-butt trick I had to perform in order to catch Coco's poop. But because I was devoted to Craig in my own way, I tried to make peace with his dog.

I noticed that when Craig and I fought, Coco hid in the bathroom. When Craig whooped for the Knicks, Coco barked. When I went to write at my desk, he came and sat at my feet. These things began to make me understand why Craig was so fond of him.

It wasn't that growing up, I hadn't liked having pets, only that aside from my cat, I'd never really bonded with the other animals, and, well, their animal-ness generally bothered me, their dirt, their lost feathers and fur, their stench, their cawing and barking, their stinky food, their awful deaths.

When I was a girl, all of our pets had met traumatic accidents. One dog drowned in a whirlpool that formed when the creek flooded. My brother's parrot opened his cage with his beak during the night and flew into Matt's bed, under the covers, which soon smothered him. My cat, hiding on top of the wheel of a neighbor's car, was run over when they backed out of the driveway. We had a white West Highland terrier, like the mustached dog in ads for Scotch whiskey. But we lived far from the chill of the Scottish Highlands, in humid Houston, Texas, where the heat and chemical fumes from the oil fields produced a skin disease in her that caused her to lose all her fur. When she died, she resembled a piglet.

Coco's gruesome habits made me think of those other pets' horrifying accidents, the raw workings of their fragile little bodies. Living with him in that tiny apartment, I could hardly ignore his animal-ness. But after some time, like roommates, Coco and I became accustomed to one another. I did the few chores required of me (half the feeding and walking), and he left me alone. I tried not to let my girly-girl fastidious-ness get the best of me.

Then one day after an upsetting phone call, I began to cry, and from another room, Coco came over to me, his tail lowered, his head cocked to the side, his happy panting paused. I was sitting on the couch, and he stood close enough to study me, but not so close that he crowded me. He leaned forward a little on his front paws, absolutely quiet. When I said his name, he took a step forward, then stopped to watch me again; I felt him trying to fathom my sorrow. There was a nar-row space between the coffee table and the couch, and he began to pace through it back and forth, offering his thick fur as if to soothe me.

❖ ❖ ❖

Strangers often mistook Coco for a puppy. He had a snout shape and mouth that curved in a way that made it seem as if he were smiling almost constantly. The husky in him gave him his ring tail, which curled up and waggled when he walked like a thick brown-and-white feather. In a city famous for its depressives, Coco beamed and pattered along the sidewalk, ears pricked up.

Each morning and afternoon when he heard the jangle of the leash, he'd leap and bark, jubilant at the prospect of a walk. He trotted down the apartment building's steps with the leash in his mouth, exuberant, as if this walk had the potential to be so much better and different from all of the others. And though we basically walked the same streets, it was true, in a way. Who knew what he'd find?

When my family is gathered at the dinner table, there is talk of which water is bad for you, how certain kinds of fat cause cancer, and how a foul-tasting herb will cleanse one's system. My father won't eat chicken, my brother won't eat fish, my other brother won't eat meat, my sister, my mother, and I only rarely will eat anything fried or chocolate. We are not good eaters. If he could have understood the situation, I'm sure that Coco would have pitied us. How narrow our options were!

Coco ate: birthday candles, cupcake wrappers, tar, an unidentifiable green sludge, possibly a dead mouse, baked beans, a certain green leaf filled with hard peas, coagulated chocolate milk, jelly beans, hot dogs, bits of red rubber, his own orange vomit.

We tried to stop him from eating anything that was bad for him, but often failed. I had to learn to survey the sidewalk and street for loose bits of food stuck through the mesh of the trash can, tiny beaks or bits of fur in the bushes, take-out food dropped in the gutter. But it was difficult to be vigilant, day after day, walk after walk. Sometimes I would stop on one of our walks to chat with someone I knew, and I'd look down to find Coco ecstatically licking the empty pavement.

Once Craig had been walking ahead of Coco, and when he looked back, there were feathers hanging from Coco's mouth. Craig tried to get him to drop the dead bird, but he wouldn't.

"Excuse me," passersby helpfully said, "but your dog has a bird in his mouth."

"I know," he said, embarrassed, thanking them, knowing there wasn't much to be done until he got Coco inside and might be able to ply him with a bribe. Cheese, if we had it.

Whenever Coco brought home something dead or a bloody bone sure to make him sick, there was a contest: Coco's devotion to Craig tested against his desire for the thing in his mouth. First, Craig tried to pry the thing from Coco's mouth, but his jaws would clamp down with super canine strength, and that never worked, though sometimes he might be able to pry away a piece of the booty. Usually, he had to take Coco upstairs to the apartment, keeping the thing in his mouth away from the furniture, and go into the kitchen, where the bribe would occur. "Wouldn't you rather have cheese, Coco? Wouldn't you rather have a dog treat?" Craig's best salesmanship skills suddenly at work for the barter.

Coco would look up, his eyes confused as he deliberated. Usually, he chose the booty he'd scavenged for himself no matter how inferior to the treat offered him, and Craig would be furious. I had a different tactic. When Coco brought home something gross or dangerous, I'd watch for the moment when he put down the thing to breathe and I'd try to grab it while he growled and snapped at me. Usually he won, the dragon in the fairy tale, claiming his treasure.

After Coco had been sick (and miraculously, he wasn't sick often), we always knew he'd recovered when he began again to go after something to put in his mouth. But often even nausea and a shaky stomach didn't deter him. Any responsible caretaker has to at times deny the desires of the cared for, but I have to say that denying Coco was particularly difficult. Once he leapt more than five feet to the back of the kitchen counter for a frozen steak. He couldn't open the refrigerator, but he was perceptive enough to angle his nose inside if anyone left the door ajar. One night when my sister was staying with him, he must have used his head to knock down a tin of expensive imported biscotti that had been sitting on a table. He ground his teeth through the tin and ate every single crumb.

Coco ate: popcorn, hair pomade, dirty kitty litter, Twinkies, red Chanel lipstick, used tea bags, spaghetti, sandalwood soap, Cheerios, orange peels, ham, cream cheese, though, oddly, never leather or shoes.

Because we were watching them, each of his bodily functions, especially his lunges for food, came to seem like a performance. Punk Rock: Coco growling and grabbing a bagel in his teeth even as I shouted "No!" Comic: Coco carrying a nail file in his mouth for blocks, refusing to accept the fact that it was tasteless. Existential: the long face and the tail lowered because the one lousy piece of stale bread had been beyond the reach of his leash.

We fed Coco what he needed to stay healthy, but he wanted more. There is something to be said for a vigorous and not-too-discriminating appetite. He wanted danger, sweetness, blood, strangeness, adventure, salt. Who could blame him? I came to see that part of the pleasure of having a dog is the empathic part, recognizing those sensitivities that we usually think of as human, but another pleasure is in a dog's beastliness. A dog acts like a dog, and I'll admit that I took a vicarious pleasure in watching Coco get the fish skin out of the restaurant's garbage. He was so happy with himself, his tail wagging, devoutly licking and savoring the luminous skin between his paws.

Much of the affection I had begun to feel for Coco came from the very things that had repelled me before. I cleaned up his vomit. I picked up his poop with a newspaper, judging whether it signaled health or sickness. I let him drag me to the cast-off Christmas tree at the curb, where he joyfully peed. Each morning, I used a lint roll to pick up the shed fur that had settled on my clothes. It wouldn't be true to say I enjoyed this work exactly—they were banal, sometimes gruesome tasks—but day after day, the work of caring for Coco made me care about him. There were times when what he scavenged seemed almost like a gift to me—a bone with a glisten of fat, a wad of dirty, aromatic foil—and I grew to love Coco, and even his appetite, for the way he reminded me daily of the pleasures of the flesh.

To be so close to the workings of a dog's body creates an intimacy that I had somehow not understood before Coco. I knew not only what he'd eaten (usually), but how much he'd enjoyed it, and whether it had made him suffer afterward. When he leapt onto my lap to beg for food, I smelled his horrible breath, felt his saliva on my cheek, the warmth and soft leatheriness of his paws, which always smelled, oddly, of turkey stuffing.

He died last year when he was sixteen years old, ancient for a dog, though he was mistaken for a puppy up until the last month of his life. I'm convinced it was his appetite that kept him young.

Years ago, one of our friends commissioned a portrait of Coco from a painter. So that the artist would have an image to work from, I took several photographs of Coco. She chose the one I'd taken at the end of one of our walks and created a remarkable likeness, even to the detail of the angles of his teeth, the faint stripe at the top of his head. At the time, it seemed precious and a bit of a joke to have a portrait of one's dog, but now I'm grateful that we have it.

Coco's face is painted in the center of a square board, with a flame-like design radiating from his head and a tongue speckled with pink polka dots. It hangs above our mantel, the style part Andy Warhol, part folk art, Coco wearing the expression he had after eating something he shouldn't have, eyes a little too bright, his mouth happily open, his face green and red, as if he's either a devil dog or one ready for Christmas, either a creature of unrestrained gluttony, or one expecting presents.

POMPEY
THE
GREAT

Chris Offutt

As a child I had the greatest dog to ever walk the earth, named Pompeius Magnus by my father. Pompey was a black-and-tan coonhound who never hunted. He arrived at our house as a puppy in a box when I was eight. He immediately made a mess on the floor. My father rubbed his nose in it and threw him in the yard. Pompey never again entered the house. I don't know where Pompey did his rearward business, but it wasn't anywhere in sight. In winter he slept outside, curled against the bottom of the brick chimney.

Within six months, Pompey began walking me to school. Because my parents preferred to remain in bed, I prepared breakfast for my younger siblings and Pompey. He received Gravy Train in a bowl mixed with water while the rest of us ate Wheaties and milk. Pompey and I followed a path beside a rain branch that dropped through the woods from the hilltop to a creek in the hollow where the Haldeman Grade School sat. He met me every afternoon after school and escorted me home through the Daniel Boone National Forest. I was never afraid of snakes, dogs, or humans as long as I was with Pompey. On weekends he slept late and roamed the woods—the same as me.

Pompey the Great protected me from other dogs on the hill, doing battle occasionally, a fearless opponent in combat. He once ripped the eyeball from a much bigger dog, a German shepherd who made the mistake of jumping on me. Pompey launched an airborne attack and clamped his jaws around the shepherd's throat. This occurred just outside the grade school one afternoon. The principal rushed from the building and smashed Pompey on the head with a coal shovel, a blow that stunned him and allowed his enemy to gain purchase and tear most of an ear away. I attacked the principal in retaliation. The German shepherd saw his chance and went for me again, exposing himself to Pompey's teeth, and that's when Pompey took the eyeball. The dogs split apart eventually, their coats slick with blood, jaws dripping saliva. The principal was astounded that a fourth-grader had struck him. For years afterward the principal gave me an uneasy respect, due without a shred of doubt to the loyalty shared between Pompey and me.

In summer I picked hundreds of ticks from his thick fur, placed their bodies on a flat rock, and smashed them with a smaller rock. Often they were swollen by blood to the size of a pea, their skin stretched and gray. I considered these ticks a prize due to the squirt of dark blood when they died. The grand prize was the female tick that had given birth to several babies, already latched to Pompey's skin beneath the mother's belly. Pompey remained docile during this grooming. He never in his life bit me, snapped at me, or growled at me. I never pulled his tail, kicked him, or hit him with a stick. I had two friends as a child—a teddy bear I slept with and Pompey the Great. Neither ever disappointed me. Everyone else in my life did.

In Haldeman, Kentucky, my hillside community of two hundred, every family owned dogs who lived outside. The majority of dogs in eastern Kentucky were a form of tool—watchdog, hunting dog, child protector. In addition, many families had a special dog who got loving treatment as a pet. These dogs accompanied people in cars, were gathered in arms, and received table scraps. None were fancy breeds. None went to a veterinarian. When Pompey came home beat up from a dogfight, my father wore leather gloves and doctored the dog while I assisted. I was rarely sick as a child, but when I was, my mother said I acted just like Pompey— I went off by myself to wait out the healing.

A neighbor across the creek once went to sleep with nine dogs and woke up with thirty-four because five of them had pups overnight. Some people abused their dogs, while other people deliberately trained their dogs to be mean. Naturally there were dogs who went feral in the woods. Those chased me and bit me. As a result, I possess excellent rock-throwing accuracy due to defending myself against charging dogs on the rare occasion that I was caught in the woods without Pompey.

Dogs who chased cars were considered a unique case, and the favored technique was to wrap your tires with old burlap bags. The fabric trapped the dogs' teeth and dragged them as long as the driver wanted. My father carried a B.B. pistol under the seat to shoot at Blackie, a neighbor's dog who chased his car. He encouraged me to keep rocks in the backseat for throwing at Blackie. Eventually my father shot Blackie from his bedroom window with a .22 rifle. He was safe since the dog was owned by an old woman who lived alone with the improbably wonderful name of Dixie Blizzard.

I have seen neighbors shoot their own dogs as punishment for erring in a crucial situation. There were no burials. Dead dogs were thrown over the hill, the same as any discarded tool. One summer, I accompanied another boy every morning to a tree where a dog was tied, and we took turns firing a small pistol near the dog's head so that it would learn not to be afraid of the sound. That same summer Pompey began killing the chickens that belonged to our neighbors. A man came to the house and warned us to tie our dog up, but no one in our family had the heart to do it. Eventually someone shot Pompey in the ass at relatively close range with a shotgun. He made it home, and my father spent several hours using a pair of pliers to pick shot out of Pompey's body. For some reason, he decided not to take Pompey to a veterinarian.

Later my father told me that the pellets had severed Pompey's testicles. Quite a bit of shot still remained inside his body. They interfered with his bowels because he never ate or shat in a normal fashion again. Some of his wounds did not fully heal. Pompey became fat. He didn't chase rabbits and squirrels anymore. He didn't accompany any of us anywhere in the woods. He smelled bad at all times. He ceased to look me in the eye. Pompey spent six months dying, finally freezing to death outside because he was still not allowed in the house.

When I asked where he was buried, my mother refused to answer me. I queried her three times. Finally she said he wasn't buried. The ground was too cold and my father had thrown his body out with the garbage. That was the last time I remember crying as a boy.

In the past few years, some people have taken me to task over my apparent callous attitude toward dogs. One of them, a Montana bird hunter named Nick Davis, remains appalled by my lack of sensitivity to dogs. Nick is a die-hard Green Bay Packers cheesehead and a former Deadhead who attended more than 150

Grateful Dead concerts. He's worked as a poker dealer, an athlete's agent, and a movie reviewer. This is a guy who walks into the Rocky Mountains carrying a loaded weapon with which he's able to knock flying birds out of the air, dutifully retrieved by Miles. When Miles died, Nick had his testicles removed and flown to Portland, Oregon, where enough sperm was extracted for a litter. Nick sent me an e-mail that said in a year he'd have "a little pupsicle."

Like many dog owners, Nick insists upon deluding himself that everyone on the face of the earth is eager to "meet" his dogs. I think of an introduction as a process limited to humans, an act with a certain formality even under informal conditions, an ancient exchange relegated by cultural traditions, social politesse, and family politics. What, I often ask Nick, is the protocol for "meeting" a dog? How does one be polite to a dog? Should I get on my hands and knees and smell the spot beneath his tail? Should I offer to shake, make small talk about the weather, inquire about the health of his family? Nick's response is that I am being ridiculous, but I think not.

Frankly, I believe that dog lovers tend to err on the side of absurdity. Some have the audacity to put their dog on the phone. Children are bad enough with the phone, but a dog is quite frankly unable to speak

English. Most won't even bark into the receiver on command. Invariably the gleeful dog owner will follow the pattern of a proud parent and leave the dog on the phone too long, as if believing that a scintillating conversation may at any moment break out. It is quite difficult to resume conversation with a human after attempting to communicate with a dog via telephone.

I once witnessed a woman calling her dog on the phone. The dog was home alone, God forbid, and the woman was worried that he was lonely, so she called her own apartment, knowing that the answering machine would pick up and she could speak to the dog in a one-sided conversation. She said that she loved him, he was a good boy, and she'd be home soon. After hanging up, she turned to me and said, "He loves that." I nodded like a moron, and it wasn't until much later that I wondered how in the hell she knew her dog loved that. It's impossible to know such information unless she rigged a video camera and played it back later. The reality is, a dog was alone in an apartment where the phone rang. Everything else existed in the imagination of my soon-to-be ex-friend.

Recently I overheard two dog owners in a small city park discussing the dreams their dogs had while sleeping. I interrupted to ask what made them believe that their dogs could dream. Both gave me patient explanations that included descriptions of their dogs' muscle twitchings, moaning as if in pursuit, and scurrying motions with the paws. When I put forth the possibility that this was merely the way dogs slept, they said in unison that they knew their dogs. They walked smugly away with their leashed pets.

I sat on a park bench and thought for a long time about the one dog I had gotten to know well. Pompey the Great never experienced a leash, a collar, or a fence. In true heroic fashion, he does not have a grave. There is no photograph of him. Pompey enjoyed a sense of utter freedom that is rarely seen in humans, let alone a dog. That liberty was his greatest gift to me, one I still retain.

I have never owned another dog.

I never will.

"THOSE DOG BEDS ARE DOPE"

T Cooper

I.
You'll never work in pictures again.

Murray is a miniature pinscher who has lived with me since he was eight weeks old. He's now eight years old. When Murray was about two, we moved to New York City and started life among the fabulous. Murray quickly fit in, becoming gay almost immediately.

Murray is a fine-looking dog. He has really nice thighs and a tight little butt, and certainly, if I can say so myself, doesn't have those bugged-out eyes that many smaller breeds tend to get. He is larger than most miniature pinschers, and in excellent shape, having been treated by me like a "big dog" his whole life.

Jobless, I sent some photos of Murray to a top animal agent in town (the agency shall remain nameless, but it starts with a "D"). They were somewhat impressed with Murray's portfolio. I had included a Birkenstock advertisement he appeared in as a pup—skillfully chewing on a mocha-colored, suede Arizona™ model sandal. He had also been accepted into the 365-dogs-a-year desk calendar, striking quite a handsome Thursday, February 4. "D" Agency said they'd call if anything came up.

I didn't hear anything from them for many months, and then Murray and I traveled to New Orleans, where we had lived prior to New York. It was a pleasant trip indeed, there being nothing more right than New Orleans in October. Murray visited with some old friends from the levee of the Mississippi River, where we went each day for an off-leash run and swim with other local dogs. Many of Murray's best friends took his coming out well, and even his ex, Sonia the rottweiler, warmed up to the fact that Murray couldn't help who he was attracted to.

Upon returning to New York, I found my answering machine blinking with several messages (I still haven't figured out how to check the damn thing from another location):

"Hi. Ms. Cooper, this is 'D' Agency. We believe we have a job for Murray next week. Please call us at your earliest convenience." Beep.

"Ms. Cooper, I don't know whether you got the last message, but we have a magazine shoot for which we're casting a miniature pinscher, and we're pretty sure your dog Murray would be perfect for it. Please call us immediately." Beep.

"This is 'D' Agency again, and we're going to have to give this job to another dog if we don't hear from you by five o'clock today. It's really too bad. This is a *Vogue* shoot." Beep.

"Ms. Cooper, thank you so much for applying for the job; we're really excited to have interviewed someone with your qualifications for the managing editor position, because this Web world—we're really confident—is really going to launch this magazine into a whole other stratosphere. But unfortunately, the position has already been filled. If any more jobs open up, by all means we'll definitely consider you." Beep.

"This is 'D' Agency again. We've already cast the *Vogue* photo shoot. Please disregard the previous messages." Beep.

I called the agency first thing in the morning. An eight-page spread in *Vogue*. The winter fashion issue. A dog walking on a leash with six or seven beautiful models—Murray could've done that, he's great at that. I mean, he pulls on the leash sometimes, but for *Vogue* . . .

"D" said not to expect a call from them again. That they like to assume their clients are both eager and available, neither of which Murray and I proved to be. In effect, that me and Murray, we couldn't expect to work in animal entertainment ever again. And worse still—the nail in the coffin, if you will—they intimated that miniature pinschers would be "out" as soon as this shoot was published anyway.

But what about Jack Russell terriers? I wanted to know. They were still going strong, and they had practically monopolized the dog market—on TV shows, commercials, in print ads. For God's sake, J. Crew models all sported Jack Russells while frolicking on the beach in the middle of winter! A Jack Russell even posed with Governor Whitman on billboards all over New Jersey, discouraging kids from smoking cigarettes. *What did Jack Russells have to do with smoking prevention?* I demanded. But "D" Agency had no answers for me; we parted professional ways as soon as they hung up on me. As I placed the phone back in its cradle, Murray came to sit next to me on the couch, looking up at me with his perfectly proportioned, doelike eyes. I could tell he was disappointed.

"We don't need them," I said, as much to myself as to Murray.

II.
"Do you want a Jack Russell Terrier because they are like Eddie and Wishbone on TV?"
—Jack Russell Terrier
Rescue Club of America Website

According to the Jack Russell Terrier Rescue Club of America, many Jack Russells come to them because they are so popular both on TV and in advertisements. Wanting one because of their popularity, however, is not such a good idea. Jack Russells are hunting dogs, prone to frantic digging, barking, jumping, aggression toward humans, and the killing of small animals. The organization does not recommend leaving them at home with other small animals like rabbits, cats, or even other small dogs. And it certainly doesn't deem them good with children.

Their Website offers a free survey to determine whether a Jack Russell is right for you: the Profiler Suitability Test. My profiler suitability rating, by the way, was a 78 (high), or four stars. It didn't indicate whether this was 78 out of 100, or four out of five possible stars, just that there is no right or wrong score, that the test is meant to make you stop and think before going out and getting a Jack Russell. My weaknesses were that I live in an apartment and not in the country. One of my strengths was that I didn't answer "yes" to the question: "Do you want a Jack Russell Terrier because they are like Eddie and Wishbone on TV?"

In a straw poll conducted by me, a majority of Jack Russell owners seemed to resent this question when it was posed to them on the street. Surprisingly, and seemingly unrelated to anything, roughly 40 percent of the dogs whose owners I polled were also named "Max." Nevertheless, here, a cross section of responses:

- ❖ "I ended up with him because my roommate's cousin left him when he moved."
- ❖ "I don't know who Wishbone and Eddie are."
- ❖ "Yeah, I guess they are really popular now, aren't they?"
- ❖ "I've been fond of JRTs since I was a small child, and we've had them in our family since my grandfather's time. He certainly wasn't influenced by television, was he?"
- ❖ "Do you have an extra bag so I can pick up after him?"
- ❖ "She's not a Jack Russell; she's a rat terrier."

III.

"French fashion designer Emanuel Ungaro's new ad campaign features a white German shepherd in a dominatrix mask, the dog licking model Kirsten Owen's feet, and, in possibly the most explicit ad, the dog mounting Owen from behind."

—*Fortune*, February 21, 2000

If 2000 was the year of the purebred dog and Christopher Guest's sleeper *Best in Show*, then 2001 was the year of the mutt. *The New York Times* Style section proclaimed: "The non-status dog has become the status dog. You now want to win Worst in Show," proving once again that even being not "in" must become "in" before anyone will take it seriously.

And nowhere was this transition reflected more than on the runways. In 2000, Chanel matched an elegant black evening gown with an ebony poodle striding alongside the bony model. In another show, a tanned, rugged Ralph Lauren model clad in a brown tweed riding jacket and brown leather pants strutted the runway with a color-coordinated basset hound. (Leather and dogs, anyone?) And of course, during the accompanying marketing blitz for the film sequel *102 Dalmatians*, Disney sent every model in its fashion show of designs inspired by the film down the runway with a purebred dalmatian pup.

But soon after the purest in canine bloodlines was brought out to help boost these designers' new lines, Ron Chereskin picked up on the *New York Times* Style section's mutt buzz and devoted his entire 2001 spring preview collection show to matching each of his hunky models with often color-coordinated mixed breeds. While the crowd went wild for the adorable dogs, surely lifting prospects for Chereskin's spring line, there was a serious side, too: All of the dogs were available for adoption from the Humane Society of New York.

The model Marcus Shenkenberg appeared with a shepherd mix, and immediately after, the Humane Society was flooded with potential do-gooders prowling the kennels in search of the same dog. Some even telephoned first to see if a dog like that was available—in effect, to see whether or not they would be interested in rescuing a dog that day, subject to availability.

When in doubt, corporate America goes to the dogs, too. The versatile, gender-bending Chihuahua Gidget was hired by Taco Bell Corp., effectively launching the breed's popularity into the stratosphere. For some time, she slung more sloppy gorditas down the throats of more customers than even Taco Bell had imagined when they hired a hotshot new advertising firm to spark sluggish sales in the first place. But by the end of 2000, folks were uttering "Yo quiero Taco Bell" no more, and Gidget was let go. (No need to worry about Gidge, though; she landed two feature film roles after Taco Bell gave her the boot.)

Enter the mongrel. Perhaps Taco Bell might've considered throwing Gidget over for a mutt: After a 22 percent drop in Gap Inc.'s profits (due in part to Old Navy's lower-than-hoped-for sales), the company launched an entire line of Old Navy fashions and products for dogs in 2001: leashes in floral prints, colorful dog bowls, designer tennis balls, pastel plaid collars, and bandannas coordinated to some of the clothing for humans in the stores. Old Navy's mascot Magic, an Airedale terrier mix and former stray, was at the helm of a brand-new advertising scheme, encouraging all scrappy dogs to take up these designer duds and move up in the world as he had. While Old Navy wouldn't comment on how the line was doing, one sales associate at an Old Navy store in mid-Manhattan gleefully reported to me, "The red bones don't sell a lot, but those dog beds are dope."

IV.

"When a celebrity has a dog, we get a lot of requests for that kind of a dog."

—Sandra DeFeo, co–executive director of the
Humane Society of New York

Matching

1. Martha Stewart   A. a mutt
2. Chris Kirkpatrick ('NSync)B. Doberman pinschers
3. Oprah Winfrey   C. bullmastiff
4. Sarah Jessica Parker D. Chihuahuas
5. Janine Turner   E. Great Dane
6. Richard Simmons F. chow chows
7. Kelsey Grammer   G. poodle
8. Mike Tyson   H. cocker spaniels

9. William Shatner   I. pug
10. Brian Littrell   J. almost 101 dalmatians
    (Backstreet Boys)

(1. F, 2. I, 3. H, 4. A, 5. G, 6. J, 7. E, 8. C, 9. B, 10. D)

V.
"If you want a friend in Washington, get a dog."
—Harry Truman

When President George W. Bush's Marine One helicopter landed on the White House lawn, it delivered him and the First Lady home from a tense, presumably strategic weekend of presumably strategizing at Camp David. The Pentagon had been ripped open and the World Trade Center leveled just weeks before.

As the doors peeled back, a black-and-white English springer spaniel named Spot exploded out of the helicopter and onto the perfectly groomed lawn below—a blur of fur. Soon the president emerged, with a black, heavy-looking, pointy-eared wiry mop of a dog in his arms and, of course, his other best friend Laura by his side. The president saluted the young marine standing at attention, while the First Lady flashed a matronly smile at him, and Barney, the newest addition to the First Family, squirmed in the president's arms in hopes of following his elder sibling Spot onto the grass.

Barney, a postelection gift to the president from his then-new environmental secretary Christine Todd Whitman, hadn't quite learned how to act in a time of conflict with a rogue Arab nation like his sister had. Spot had, in fact, been born in the White House, a bona fide second-generation resident. She was one of many pups of Millie Bush, the best-selling author and former First Dog of President Bush Senior and his best friend Barbara.

Barney, a Scottish terrier and clearly the black sheep in the family (barring Jeb), greeted the line of press awaiting the president's arrival, as Spot disappeared into the White House. "Mr. President, what is your response to the Taliban's latest offer to try bin Laden in Afghanistan?"

Bush stopped, dropping his wife's hand. The look on his face changed from respectful and contemplative to pissed off and without TelePrompter, as he crossed toward the unruly network of microphones before him.

"No negotiations!" the president demanded. "When I said no negotiations, I meant no negotiations."

"So you're rejecting the offer," et cetera, et cetera—a cacophony of questions from the distinguished members of the press.

"I don't know what the offer is. All they got to do is turn him over."

"They want you to stop the bombing."

"Barney! Come 'ere, Barney!" he called. "They must not have heard, there's no negotiations. This is non-negotiable."

More questions.

"What are you—what's he *doing* over there?" the president demanded. "Come on, Barney! Get out of there."

The president smiled—that smile where your dog is doing something embarrassing while you're supposed to be being the leader of the world's only remaining superpower. "No negotiations. There's no need to negotiate. Period. Come *on*, Barney!"

Flashbulbs flashed. The president ignored the further questions. He waited until finally Barney came, scooting into the White House with the president shaking his head and following after—strangely, no more able to control his dog than the rest of us.

VI.

"Now that his master was gone he was lying neglected on the heaps of mule and cow dung that lay in front of the stable doors . . . and he was full of fleas. As soon as he saw Odysseus standing there, he dropped his ears and wagged his tail . . . but Argos died as soon as he had recognized his master."

—Homer, *The Odyssey,* Book XVII

In hopes of finding a horror story about a dalmatian who had been purchased in one of the frenzies brought on by the Disney live-action film *101 Dalmatians* and its sequel *102 Dalmatians,* I sent one tiny e-mail to Save the Dalmatians, a Southern California–based breed rescue organization. Instead of one horror story, however, my e-mail in box was flooded with well over fifty, and that was just in the first two days after my request. And some of these fifty had adopted two and three dalmatians apiece.

Save the Dalmatians, along with literally hundreds of other dalmatian rescue organizations in this country and others, almost single-handedly cleaned up the mess that the Disney films and accompanying marketing bonanzas sparked. Or, I should say, they cleaned up the remaining mess after the shelter systems did their requisite part of the cleanup effort: putting down thousands of unwanted, injured, and abused dalmatians. In Southern California alone, it's estimated that more than ten thousand dalmatians came through all of the area shelters in 1999; the vast majority of these dogs were killed.

Rescuers of dalmatians, or dals, as breed aficionados call them, are a plucky bunch, with an air about them somewhat akin to soldiers engaged in years of confounding trench warfare. They want to help get the word out, but just don't spell it *dalmation*. Hell hath no fury like a dalmatian fancier angered by an *o* instead of an *a*. Cathy Murphy of Touchstone Dalmatians writes:

> PLEASE learn to spell the name of our breed CORRECTLY! The name is DALMATIAN, NOT dalmation! This is a very sore point among knowlegable [sic] DalmatiAn breeders. If you cannot at least spell the name of the breed Correctly, you certainly don't know much of anything about the breed."

Admittedly, a few of the dozens of other rescuers corrected my spelling, but only after sharing their stories and thanking me for asking. Many of these people included their full addresses, home and work telephone numbers, cell phones, and, in two instances, their fax numbers. And I won't even get started on the number of attached photos of spotted dogs I received. Or the e-mail from the man with colon cancer, whose dalmatian was narrowly rescued from death at the pound and is now the only reason the man gets up and out of bed every morning. The doctor tells him those two walks a day could be extending his life.

There is this entire world out there, folks who have inherited the flesh-and-blood residue from a multimillion-dollar PR job that essentially said, "Dalmatians = cute, cuddly, obedient & great addition to the family." Backyard breeders, looking to turn a buck, proliferated the market with often poorly bred puppies, and then uninformed, impulsive consumers bought them up. Cardboard signs were posted on telephone poles all over Everytown, USA: DALMATIAN PUPPIES—$250. When little Susie sees Pongo and Perdy bouncing across the screen at Christmastime, does Daddy really call the number on the sign and then go out and buy a black-and-white-spotted puppy from some guy who lives at the end of a cul-de-sac, with gut-wrenching howls and the thick stench of various forms of elimination issuing from his property? Yep. It's for the kids. The kids!

Dalmatian puppies—no matter how well or poorly bred—grow to be big, hyper, strong, and often deaf. They need at least thirty minutes of rigorous exercise a day. The dogs should be obedience trained because of their strength and energy. Dalmatians can escape most yards, may whine and bark excessively if left alone, and for some and all of these reasons, frustrated owners often deem them just plain stupid. Irresponsible and sloppy breeding with the ultimate goal of churning out large numbers of puppies just in time for, say, a Christmas launch of a film only compounds these problems.

One such backyard breeder, as they are known, had a litter of mostly dalmatian-looking puppies in the panhandle of Florida. When some of the white pups didn't start getting spots, he killed two of them and kept two who looked like they might eventually develop some. Promising that the spots would come in at six months, the breeder managed to sell one of these puppies to a customer, who later dumped the puppy at the local pound—yes, because of the lack of spots, but also because the dog grew "too big and hyper." The breeder himself dropped off the remaining spotless dog at the pound, because he couldn't sell it. Perhaps it had grown too large for him to kill himself, so he wanted to let someone else do it for him. That dog was rescued before being put down; the new owner obedience trained her, and she now works as both a therapy dog and a blood donor at a veterinarian hospital where transfusions are performed on critically ill animals. All this, with just a few spots.

Then there was the puppy in Orange County, California, who was bought just before Christmas, but he whined a lot at night before going to sleep. The kids had begged for a dalmatian after seeing the film, but after about a week they had scratches on their hands and arms, and they complained to their father that the puppy played too rough. When it came time to visit relatives for the holidays, there was no way an unruly puppy was going to come along on the road trip. So they left him in the kitchen, with a door open to a bathroom—he could drink out of the toilet—and a big bowl of food on the floor. Only the food ran out, and the puppy couldn't reach the toilet. Dad dropped him off at the pound shortly after the family returned from their trip. The puppy arrived covered in his own feces and urine, dehydrated and starved. He had been wrapped in a towel and transported in a large shopping bag. He died the next morning, before the local dalmatian rescue organization could even get there.

And there are rumors of another *103 Dalmatians* to look forward to.

VII.
Those who can, do, and those who can't, complain.

A month after Murray and I were blacklisted in the fashion industry, I picked up a copy of the holiday issue of *Vogue*. Sure enough, there was the other miniature pinscher, strutting down a tree-lined Greenwich Village street with bundled-up models practically fawning all over him. Brown was the new black that year. The little dog's leash was taut, and he clearly wasn't present in his role. He obviously hadn't considered his motivation for the scene at all. Entirely wrong for the part. Plus, his eyes really bugged out.

FEAR OF THE OTHER

Pearl Abraham

Several weeks after my dachshund Emma came into my life, I woke with her long tail curled beside me, black-and-tan fur on the white linen of my bed, and knew as I hadn't before, that I was living with something quite other, a demon out of I. B. Singer's stories. I felt thrilled and menaced simultaneously.

In Jewish folktales of my childhood demons and dybbuks, disguised as dogs and cats, enter the body of a child and possess it. In some stories, demons present themselves as women, therefore men are advised to check suspect wives for tails and webbed feet, the give-away signs of the demonic or not human. And in the city of Jerusalem, where in 1967, when I lived there, cats were as numerous as field mice in a cornfield, the prevailing superstition that touching a dog or cat causes a loss of memory and with it all one's Torah learning was often repeated in warning.

Biblical law makes ownership of a domesticated dog or cat redoubtable, too. Carnivorous animals—Emma is a mouse and rabbit killer—fall into the category of contaminants. In ancient times, contact with a contaminant required purification, a cultic ritual that called for a seven-day separation from the tribe, followed by a thorough washing in water stirred with the ashes of a rare red cow. Though this singular cow is no longer obtainable, such purification rituals endure among orthodox Jews in modified forms.

Given these taboos, it's no surprise that I grew up afraid of dogs. My first experience with a dog took place when I lived for a summer with my family in a Catskills bungalow colony whose owner had a large black Lab. Years later I can still remember the nightmare of Ahab, who would arrive out of nowhere and corner us in vulnerable places, on a swing not high enough off the ground, in the swimming pool, or walking home from the canteen. A lumbering lummox, he would bound toward us with what was surely playful delight, and which we perceived as murderous zeal. A scene from that summer begins with my siblings and me running from the swing set, leaving behind the youngest to Ahab (it's only in writing this that the connection with the fictional Ahab occurs to me), who snatches at her underpants with his teeth, a sentimental image out of Norman Rockwell turned by our terror into something Munch-like. To make matters worse, our mother to whom we ran for help was frighteningly helpless, paralyzed by her own fear of dogs.

As an adult, my experience with dogs was also limited. In one instance a friend who was dog-sitting a yappie Yorkie named Buck asked me to take Buck for the night to allow for a last-minute date. Every time

Buck shook himself, I startled awake to the strangeness of this rattle in the night, and remained awake for hours. In the morning, first thing, I walked Buck across the park and home, never admitting that it wasn't Buck's yappiness that I minded. Several years later, this friend adopted a Jack Russell and my efforts to appear comfortable around her, "cool," so to speak, paid off. I became more comfortable.

And Flory made the question of friendship beside the point. She assumed it. In the car she insisted on sitting in my lap. In the street, she pulled me to the park. She obeyed when I told her to sit (especially if a reward seemed possible), barked when she wanted to play. Over a period of five years, she slept in my bed several times, warming my toes, and I found myself enjoying her company. Through all this, I wasn't entirely unafraid of her jaws. Rather than risk getting too close, I would toss her a treat, which she was very good at catching in the air. When at the end of a particularly lonely period (I was writing my second novel) I decided that the company of a dog would help, that it would be good to have a reason to go out every day, my experience with Flory was a deciding factor.

She and her owner came with me to Strouds-bourg, Pennsylvania, to meet the litter of dachshunds, of which Emma was the independent one, unafraid to

stray from her breeder's ankles and explore the boundaries of the kitchen, curiously sniffing at the door that
led to the outdoors. Two hours later, during her first
venture into the great wide world, we stopped at
McDonald's and tiny, three-pound Emma found her
first french fry in the grass, held on to it, and I learned
how sharp puppy teeth can be. As in all things, famil-
iarity dislodges fear.

It was some time before I informed my family
about Emma. I began by introducing her to my sister.
In conversation with her, strangely enough, I referred
to Emma as Yenty, and we laughed. The slip of the
tongue was revealing. That's what you should have
named her, my sister said.

This Yiddish word translates as *a gossip* or *busybody,*
sometimes a *tattletale*, and these comically pejorative
meanings could suit a dachshund, whose short legs and
snooping snout bring smiles to many faces. People, age
four to ninety-four, find themselves unable to walk by
without naming her: hot dog, wiener, sheine sausage.
Among well-named dachshunds, I've met a Satchel and
a Piglet; Yentl seems to me similarly right, for both
sound and sense.

Unlike the names Satchel and Piglet, Yentl is in everyday use as a human appellation, at least in my family, which makes it inappropriate for a dog, again, in my family. The name trips off my tongue so easily perhaps because Emma, much as my youngest sister Yenty once did, brings my maternal instincts to the surface.

Yenty entered our family late, when my sister and I were in our teens, and suddenly our mother was pregnant again, after an eight-year hiatus. It was a difficult pregnancy for a forty-three-year-old woman who'd already given birth eight times. As the eldest daughters help was expected of us, and we fulfilled these expectations more or less. But when informed that if the baby turned out to be a girl she would be named after our recently deceased grandmother, we balked. Even in the Yiddish-speaking world, the name is considered unattractive, and we were convinced that a child named Yentl would grow up emotionally scarred. We used every argument against the name, including the biblical one.

In Genisis, the world is created with names. The biblical word for "heaven" comes into existence before heaven itself, which suggest that to become what it has been called, heaven takes direction from its name. This process can be broken down to smaller parts. The alphabetic letters that make up the word for "earth" are brought together to form the word, and then earth has to fulfill itself within this particular combination of letters. This mystical idea that *In the beginning was the word* runs counter to everything we know about the brain and the evolution of the linguistic process. On an irrational level, however, the idea retains an element of truth in the way folk wisdom does: People have a way of growing into their names.

Several months later the child was born and named, and after her first day at home, we were all in love. Indeed, as the months passed, little Yenty gave the detested name a certain glow. Fifteen years later, my siblings, who married and became parents, each have a Yenty of their own, bringing this shtetl-world name into the twenty-first century. In Chassidic communities of New York, Yenty is known as an Abraham name. More to the point, to our minds, the name has become synonymous with *pretty*, *smart*, *talented*, all the wonderful traits one observes in one's own, which suggests that the potential for transformation is bi-directional. In the right circumstances, even the homely can acquire a certain aesthetic.

For the naming of man and animal, the biblical order is reversed. Man is first made, then named. And

Adam receives the great creative task of naming the animals created by God. Since Genesis is an origin myth, the names are prototypes, names of a species rather than particular members of that species.

The midrash tells us that Adam's task of naming the animals gave him dominion over them. Indeed, if to name a thing requires knowing it fully and if to know a thing is to triumph over it, then it was knowledge that gave Adam this dominion. But are the subsequent names we give our animals born of any knowledge? More controversially, does the goal of dominion have any relevance in our times, when presumably every dog lover supports the idea of animal rights? And what do we do with the fact that in the animal kingdom, unbenign dominion continues to rule?

That we give our dogs human names is a small manifestation of our tendency to ascribe to other species, to God even, our own attributes, and exposes our limited ability to imagine the other. Spinoza writes that a triangle would think, if it were capable of thinking, that God is a triangle. We are fallible and unknowing, and come upon knowledge with difficulty, sometimes via a lucky slip of the tongue.

I named Emma for Mrs. Peel of *The Avengers,* and also for a favorite Jane Austen character, in tribute to my early infatuation with girl sleuths and other adventurous women, beginning with Nancy Drew and moving on to include without much discrimination between the fictional and real: Trixie Belden, Cherry Ames, the Dana Girls, the British St. Clare twins, Madame Curie, Amelia Earhart, Charlie's Angels, and Emma Peel. The caprice of Emma as Yenty, or more to the point, Emma rather than Yenty, sustains my interest for what it discloses.

Before Emma, I'd named some fictional characters. I'd given titles to several books, and also to some short pieces. When for the first time, I had the real thing in front of me, the God-like opportunity to name a live being, not just an imagined figure, I chose the name of a television character. Although I couldn't have explained it at the time, I understand that Emma's name is based in the fictional world because Emma herself is an aspect of my invented life, rather than the one given to me at birth. Like the romance of life as a writer of fiction, the image of a girl with a dog is one I came to know in my life away from my family.

Though she may never meet her, my mother is fascinated in the details of life with Emma: what she eats, where she sleeps, whether she bites, her habits of hygiene, and so on. When I offered to take her along for a visit, my mother agreed. Five minutes later, the phone rang and my father requested that I leave Emma

at home. "We have neighbors," he said. "There are children in the yards and street. They'll see and hear her.
And what if she hurts someone?"

I could have told him that Emma is all of thirteen
pounds and gentle, but I know that my father, who was
raised on a farm, isn't physically afraid of animals. What
I heard in his voice was the age-old rabbinic suspicion
of the new and strange, of the other. Ironically, his fears
are similar to, perhaps the result of, the superstitious
anxieties manipulated by murderers throughout history.
To demonize the Jews, the Crusaders, the church, the
Nazis played on the primitive dread of the strange
other, as do today's Islamic terrorists.

Demonization of the other is also the source of
my mother's fears for my personal safety in my life away
from the orthodox Jewish community, in a city of many
Jews, but also many who aren't Jewish, including the
man I live with in whom she would place no trust.
She's convinced that husbands who aren't Jewish beat
their wives.

As a member of a different species, Emma is a
more extreme example of the other, and it occurs to
me to wonder how much her other-ness has to do with
her presence in my life. Close up, in my own home and
bed, I can come to know her, subdue fear. To what end?
I ask myself. Perhaps it is an attempt to return to fearless, full life in the garden of Eden before the fall.

❖ ❖ ❖

About real life with this extreme other, I'm willing to admit that it has elements of a parent–child relationship. Emma has me, like any good parent, on a strict schedule. In the morning, she gets me out of bed for her feeding. In the afternoon, she informs me that she's due for her walk.

She walks with her head high, eyes forward, determined; on this day she will catch a squirrel. I walk behind her, burdened by the knowledge that in less than an hour this walk will come to an end and with it Emma's favorite hour of the day. But Emma understands time differently, and shows me that the human way is not always best. She too knows that at some point in the future the walk will end, but this fact doesn't prevent her from taking full pleasure in the ephemeral present. She lives life fully. For the next forty-five minutes, she hunts with a single-mindedness that puts my efforts in life to shame.

At five, like clockwork, Emma stands at her bowl ready for her evening meal. In the fall, when in accordance with the Daylight Saving Time agreement we all fell behind an hour, Emma refused to adjust. She knows better. She knows that old dogs don't have to learn new tricks, and continues to stand at her bowl at five every afternoon, even if by my watch it's only four.

SPARKY

Brent Hoff

O kay. Granted it is annoying when people compare other people to animals. I have occasionally, and by people I love, been compared physically to a duck. That sucks. But truth hurts and Captain Ramos is decidedly owl-esque. Perched behind the wheel, his small head bobs and swivels atop a tubby contourless body. Bulging eyes dart out of pale sockets after scurrying pedestrians, bike mes- sengers, cabs, and all the potential disasters we are careening toward. He even hoots "Hoot! Hoot! Hoot!" along to the hyperfrenetic, coked-up Tito Puente salsa tapes he buys on Canal Street and blasts from the crappy boom box at his feet.

We are going to die. Ramos takes all forty-two feet of Ladder Truck #12 around a blind tight Financial District corner at thirty-five miles an hour, missing a peanut vendor's cart and an oncoming UPS truck by what I calculate to be one-quarter of an inch on either side. A block ahead a young pin-striper is crossing the street. The guy is either deaf, suicidal, or believes him-self invincible because he steps off the curb without even a glance toward the siren-screaming, flashing red death machine bearing down on him. I hear myself making some sort of noise. Ramos doesn't slow or blink. Our passing draft literally blows the headphones off the guy's head. In the rearview mirror he sits stunned on the sidewalk while a fellow pedestrian pulls pieces of his iPod out of the gutter.

These near-disasters occur rhythmically, block by tire-screeching, obscenity-screaming New York City block, but Captain Ramos keeps singing. Terrorizing people is his job and he loves his job. "Don't look so scared my friend!" he yells. It's true. I can hardly bear to look out the window at the bad teen movie this ride has become. God only knows what's coming next. A parade of nuns, a family of ducks? Old Italian ladies carrying laundry? I hold on to the other firefighter riding up front with us for comfort.

If I am duck-like and Ramos is owl-like then the firefighter I am clinging to is positively bovine. Stick legs, rotund body, ears jutting straight out, and large black spots on his side, Sparky is Engine #12's beloved mascot and aging fire dog and right now he seems as scared as I am. He shakes noticeably, whines loudly, digs his nails into the red pleather seat, and tries to avoid smashing his nose against the dashboard whenever Ramos grudgingly slams on the brakes. I tighten my arm around Sparky's ample middle to comfort and steady him, I rattle his head with my free hand and whisper Japanese haiku in his ear, but he is inconsolable.

Sparky is the most un-dalmatian dalmatian I have ever met. I thought he was sick or depressed the first time I met him. He just seemed so lethargic. When I commented on this back at the station, one of the guys just shrugged and said, "He's a lazy son of a bitch, what can we do?" Apparently there had been repeated attempts to get Sparky in shape but Sparky refused to run, jog, wog, or even trot more than a block. The few dalmatians I've known are all hyperfrenetic loveballs, terminally sweet, yappie as hell, and bouncy to the point of levitation, so a lazy beef-burger like Sparky is a rare sight. But who am I to stereotype dalmatians when I myself have a ninety-pound pit bull at home who utterly and completely defies his canine canon?

People are always labeling dogs as *this type* of dog or *that type* of dog. Rottweillers are so _____, hound dogs are so _____. It's racist. Yes. The world is full of dog racists. And I confess I used to be one myself.

Three years ago my girlfriend, the mean one who says I look like a duck, started browsing animal rescue shelter Websites like it was Internet porn. She would spend all day at work surreptitiously viewing photos of potential adoptees, obsessively reading their tragic life stories, and tearfully choosing her daily favorites. At night she would give me the ASPCA hard sell. I wasn't entirely against "rescuing" a dog, but I told her in no uncertain terms that I *refused* to let some abused, deranged pit bull into the apartment. It just seemed too dangerous. Pit bulls were basically four-legged sharks—dead-eyed, swivel-headed monsters with savage locking jaws, impervious to pain and scientifically bred by Nazis and/or drug dealers to crave the blood of the innocents. Who wants that kind of thing roaming around your house while you sleep? I mean, isn't that the whole point of civilization, to diminish the likelihood of being torn to shreds by wild beasts in the middle of the night? I swore if she brought home some abused pit bull I would retaliate by populating the apartment with poisonous snakes—if only to hasten our imminent deaths.

I admit I didn't trust Lugo for a long time. He had, like many pit bull puppies, been terribly abused. "Someone threw him in the East River," the hardened woman from the ASPCA told us. "We see it a lot. If a pit won't fight, the assholes try to drown them." Evidently a passing tugboat had rescued the six-month-old Red Nose, and a few months of gunpowder-free meals (don't ask) had put him on the mend. We'll never know if they threw the whole litter in or just him. Regardless, within weeks the monster was not only in our apartment, but sleeping in our bed, his shark-esque jaws inches from my face.

He seemed nice enough. Nevertheless, during the next year I kept on guard, waiting for this large pink-nosed pup to reveal his secret, evil pit bull nature. I expected the worst. I expected him to suddenly snap one day while being petted and bite my arm off. I expected him to lunge out and devour that small child passing by. I had learned that "those assholes" sometimes teach their pits "kill words"—words that send seemingly nice pits into bloody jaw-crushing attack mode. As we walked around town I nervously waited to discover Lugo's kill word. *What will it be?* I wondered. Something in German? Better stay away from tourists. A nursery rhyme? Stay away from new mothers. The name of a Yankee pitcher, a Mets catcher? Avoid guys in baseball hats. What? Any moment could be our last.

After we—yes, we—adopted Lugo, life changed. It became immediately apparent that we were now members of an exclusive club, a secret society involving all abused pit bull owners within eyesight. The Abused Pit Bull Defenders of America. To be a member all you had to do was find us, share your pit's heartbreaking life story, and then curse "the assholes." That's it. It is a very informative club. I learned many facts, like the fact that pit bulls were once, back in the 1930s, deemed the ideal family dog, à la Little Rascals. I learned that the locking-jaw business was a total myth, as was the pit's supposed inability to feel pain. And from one particularly passionate member I learned that by far the highest percentage of severe bites each year come not from pit bulls but rather from those damn cocker spaniels and that I should watch out for those psychotic little Jack Russells as well. I learned a lot from Lugo too. Walk by carnage-free walk, night by uneventful night, Lugo taught me what a dog racist I had been, and what a farce the notion of dog breeding is.

But don't take my word for it, just look at my freaked-out fire dog friend, Sparky. Dalmatians are considered the world's only "coaching breed." (As in, *large horse-drawn carriage*.) For thousands of years dalmatians have been "bred" to travel with humans. Some of the earliest drawings adorn ancient Egyptian pottery and show suspiciously spotted canines running alongside war chariots. Somewhere along the way dalmatians were adopted by bands of gypsies and traveled all over Europe alongside their caravans, protecting the lusty accordion-wielding nomads from all who would ravage their women and steal their hash. In the eighteenth century, dalmatian ancestors were imported to England as attack dogs, sporting dogs, shepherd dogs, rat catchers, bird dogs, retrievers, stag hunters, and even clown dogs in traveling circuses. Eventually English lords and ladies started traveling with dalmatians. Sparky's great-great-great-great-grandfather probably spent his days, ears entirely cropped away, a huge padlocked brass collar around his neck, running his ass off in front of some aristocrat's carriage clearing the road of peasants. And on and on until, with this long résumé as the ideal coaching breed, dalmatians landed the prestigious fire dog gig.

In Manhattan in the 1800s, fire departments were basically just gangs of drinking buddies. Even the fancy uptown firehouses, the ones the Rockefellers and Kennedys belonged to, were just a bunch of frat boy boozers. It's true. These protozoan firemen initially started keeping dalmatians around to guard the equipment and horses and chase away the rats. But being generally quick and smart and all that, their responsibilities grew to include guide, siren, house mascot, and occasionally, legend has it, heroic rescuer of babies.

Back then, a fire truck was several fast horses pulling a big barrel of water called a "pumper." When an alarm sounded, barking dalmatians charged out ahead of the fire wagon to clear other wagons, other dogs, and everyone else out of the way. Just like they did for the consumptive rich people in England but for a good cause this time. Dalmatians were able to find a fire's origin on a smoke-filled street, while the horses could just follow their black-and-white spots through the dense smoke. It worked perfectly.

(Actually, there was a little more to it than that . . . Usually several volunteer departments covered any given area. The various departments would compete to be the first wagon at a fire so they could strike a deal with the owner of the burning building. Basically the pitch went, "Hey pal [New Yorkers always say "Hey pal"], your house is on fire and we've got a water pump, how much are you gonna pay us to put it out?" If you paid them enough the men doused your house with the hose. If you couldn't pay, then it was "So long, good luck with that pail." Often, when fires struck good neighborhoods, several volunteer fire department wagons would arrive at the same time and a bloody street fight would ensue over who had dibs while the house burned to ashes. The dogs would guard the wagon from thieves while the boys were brawling or would join in depending on their mood. Departments were always getting disbanded by the police.)

Eventually horse-drawn wagons were replaced with combustion engines but dalmatians still stayed on as mascots. So what we have is literally thousands of years of humans breeding dalmatians for "purity" as a coaching breed to run alongside Egyptian chariots, gypsy carts, English carriages, and American fire wagons, and what is the end result? The end result is a chubby, frightened little cow-dog named Sparky who hates running and looks poised to vomit on my lap. That, my friends, is what all our tampering with nature has achieved, and that is why dog breeding is such a bad joke.

Yet the racism continues. My first trip to the dog run with Lugo was a festival of dirty looks and angry comments. "Keep that pit away from my dog!" a woman (a very carrion-esque woman, I might add) said when Lugo walked too close to her vizsla. Within two months that same woman had become Lugo's biggest supporter. "Don't worry, that's Lugo. He's a good pit," she would tell people. But some will never be swayed. I began to get upset with the amount of unprovoked vitriol hurled at Lugo and pit bulls in general.

One day I saw a preview for a typically absurd Fox program called *When Good Pets Go Bad!!,* which showed a vicious pit bull trying to eat the camera. Meanwhile, an exact replica of the killer pit on TV was hiding under my stairs having just developed an overwhelming fear of flies. It became clear that I had been duped by the hype.

My first glimpse into the true mind of a pit bull came just a week after my . . . hmmm, let me see . . .

after my very squirrel-like girlfriend brought Lugo home. At the exact moment I realized we had left this devil dog alone upstairs with our cat, we heard a loud yelp and I flew upstairs expecting carnage. Instead I saw Lugo standing at the foot of the bed with our cat's claw stuck completely through his eyelid. She was on the bed and must have swatted at him for getting too close. Now they were stuck and neither of them knew what to do. Where was the killer instinct? I wondered. Where were the snapping jaws of death? I carefully removed the claw and that was it.

Anyone who met Lugo and saw how unstereotypical he was would immediately claim he "must be mixed with something." It isn't surprising I guess. Every twenty years a new dog breed goes up on America's Most Feared Breed poster. It was Doberman pinschers during World War II, German shepherds after that, rottweilers for a while, and today it's the dreaded pit bull. Sure there are abused pit bulls out there who snap and kill people, but all one has to do is look at Sparky here to see how ridiculous the idea of effectively "breeding" dogs for any specific purpose is.

The fact is the whole idea of "purebred dogs" only came about in eighteenth-century Europe. That's when

powder-faced barons and baronesses decided they
needed yet one more way to display their superiority
over the commoners. *(The other popular method at the
time being the feigning of tuberculosis symptoms, the trendy
new disease that was taking artists by storm. Thus, if I have
tuberculosis, I must be very artistic.)* The not-at-all-subtle
takeaway from dog breeding being that, if some dogs
are inherently more pure than other dogs, then mightn't
the same be true for humans?

In 1870, with the establishment of kennel clubs in
Britain and America, the idea of breeding for purity
really took off. That was when "closed breeding books"
were first introduced. Thereafter a dog could be registered in a breeding book as a purebred only if both parents were registered as "pure." Soon everyone who was
anyone wanted to purge the world of "weakling" dogs
and maintain "pure bloodlines." One of the main advo-
cates for dog breeding was in fact a man by the name of
Leon Fradley Whitney who wrote a book quaintly titled
The Case for Sterilization. Leon's book argued for denying stupid people the right to have children. (He later
received fan mail for his book from another renowned
proponent of maintaining pure bloodlines, Adolf Hitler.)
This kind of bell curve shit is exactly why dalmatians
came to be used as fire dogs in the first place, and is,
unfortunately, why Sparky is so unhappy right now.

❖ ❖ ❖

As if on cue, Ramos slams on the brakes in front of a smoking building, sending Sparky's nose hard into the dashboard and my body slamming against the seat belt. "Sorry Sparks!" Ramos yells as he jumps out to join the rest of his crew at the scene. Left in the truck, Sparky immediately relaxes. He curls up on the seat, looks up at me, and lets out an absolutely relieved sigh. I think to myself, *He knows, he knows. Dalmatians are smart that way.* By playing dumb and being a lazy cuss, I believe, Sparky is attempting to single-handedly change a thousand years of tradition. If he succeeds, then in another thousand years maybe dalmatians will be viewed as the world's best "sit in the house eating fat pieces of steak" dog. Let some other breed be the official fire dog for a while. Let some weimaraner get his ears and tail pulled by bratty kids at school fire safety seminars for a change. Let some prissy poodle risk his life as Captain Ramos's copilot. Go ahead Sparky, get fat and start a trend. It's time those prancy chows got off their asses anyway.

GIRL DOG MOM

Terese Svoboda

Some say owner, some are so P.C. as to say "companion," but I've always been Mom. My first girl dog, of the breed best known as Brat Terrier, calls me Mom plenty. Can't you just hear it? Ours is a mother–daughter thing, despite her open-gendered "Spot," despite the afternoons when she chews off her pink bow until it looks way butch, so not-girl I forget and say "Bad boy, don't eat the knot, it'll give you an Adam's apple." What's a mother to do?

You think you can start over with a dog, correct all the mistakes your mother made with you. A dog will sit, after all. But just when your girl dog seems all you've ever hoped for, a sweet fluffy ball asleep in your lap, kisses whenever, she tears off after a Harley, goes stubbornly anorexic or refuses all food but steak, or worse, won't come when you call unless *you* beg. The dog is all daughter. You don't notice the terrible truth until you hear yourself saying: "We do not sniff Freddy's crotch every time he comes around," or "Eat every bit of that kibble if you want your ice cream, or Keep your damn just-shampooed hide out of that dead fish guck." Correct those mistakes? You're Mom all over again.

But maybe what you really want in a dog-daughter is not obedience to every good-for-her command but a free agent, a dog who chooses you as a woman's best friend, the one creature in the world who will always understand you, somebody just like yourself. You've seen them—Mother plays doubles with daughter, daughter tells her the real reason her boyfriend brings her home late, they turn up carrying the same handbag. People are always noticing the resemblance between Spot and myself—her spots match my basic shade of platinum that, in the time between touch-ups, reveals a lot of the same dirty brown that covers the rest of Spot. In general, our hairdos are very similar too—we both always need combing. Still, when it comes to the girl-dog-in-love scene, I forget all that palsy-walsy stuff—I revert to Mom in an instant. Spot is always trailing some Doberman who could eat her for lunch, and never the nice poodle who is more her size and style. "Do I have to leave you at home?" I shout. "When are you going to get the idea?" I'm not as bad as the woman in the dog run who speed-reels her lady dachshund after the first male sniff. Did the stud Lab twist a waxed mustache and mutter, *I almost got her that time?* Then again, that Lab might not have been as fixed as he could have been, dog runs being what they are. I have taken all the proper precautions. I knew that Spot would want wooing, given that she insists on face-licking every hound she meets. More than once I found her dragging some young thing around by his collar or biting him in some telltale unladylike way. I fixed her so fast we didn't even have time for that chat about Tampax. Sure, I mourn the loss of 1,001 litters of adorable, beautiful puppies but I have just enough sense to know that adorable is temporary and not always hereditary, especially after a surprise courtship with a corgi in the vet's waiting room. That's where I remember my mother's reaction to Rick, the cute guy with all the tattoos, the pierced and bared navel—she wasn't fishing around her purse for a cigarette, she was looking for the leash.

Sometimes I want Spot to be her own dog and not follow me everywhere, kitchen to living room to kitchen, I want her not to whine and mope when that dashing beagle down the hall goes out, I want her to forget chewing the heirloom socks. In short, I want her to grow up. Seven years for each year of mine still seems a long time to be yelling "Heel." It means she'll be Mom's age in just eight or nine years—and then what? If I know Spot, she'll sleep on the sofa all day and have crotchety opinions about squirrels and pigeons, and when I want her to growl "Hands off, buddy" at an overly amorous date, she'll just wag, hoping he'll notice her. Mom never tells me to grow up because I suspect she wants to keep age between us. She can still pull rank that way, wag her finger at me and tell me I'll never learn.

Well, I showed her I never will learn. First, I found myself hanging around the shelter, actually taking detours to press my face against the window, not just threatening Spot with a permanent stay. Was I pining after puppies? I am the eldest in a litter of nine myself, no stranger to infants of my own stripe, and I am not so excited about diaper changing aka training. I had no intention of starting over. But Spot keened whenever I left her—you'd think I threatened to abandon her in a department store—and got hysterical if I had to excuse myself from our ball-throwing and stick-hiding and actually go to work. I just wanted Spot to be happy. My happy is clearly not hers; she doesn't get all that excited about a movie deal, just banana nut ice cream. While I'm partial to certain ice creams, I am also Mom. We have to make a living to buy that next gallon, don't we? Maybe I was looking for a dog for my dog.

Behind the bars of the shelter sleeps the most beautiful Aussie with a gray, black, and white coat so stunning that fur activists must surely protect her. Some slight malformation of the hind feet has kept her from life as a show dog and condemned her to death as a dump dog. The staff says she is a dream, perfectly well behaved, fully trained and housebroken. She doesn't even bark. Having a good dog can improve the behavior of a bad one, they tell me. In no time, they promise, Spot and the Aussie will make a perfect dog-duo, they will wear each other out, there will be no long walks to the dog run and no woeful eyes following my every move pleading for those long walks, and the two dogs will love me twice as much.

I say sure.

I can't name them both Spot, even though the Aussie's fur is twice as mottled. I decide on Io, something from Greek mythology, a little classy, a little high-tech, I/O, input/output. They attend dog-training review, how to meet and greet, how not to strangle on their leashes when they see another dog (they never teach beg anymore—too demeaning?), how to forget about car-chasing. And what do they do their first week after? They leap bookcases with a single bound, they tear phone books in two like they were tissue, they bag squirrels while I am bagging and tossing out their shit. They are competitive, just like my sister with me. Oh, yes, they do learn from each other. In no time at all, Io walks with her noble head held low, a precise copy of Spot's all-out snarf position, and together they tour the neighborhood for murderous sharp pork chop bones, alert for the least stray noodle or tiny bagel crumb that might waft or could waft to the ground. A loose tea bag, the string hanging from Io's muzzle, indicates how far she has fallen. Walking them reveals distinctly different sets of interests: One wants to herd, the other wants a rat hole. They shoot off in opposite directions, one trips me, the other jerks my handbag to the ground. Or else they rush forward, ever vigilant to the possibility that one might get in front of the other. One of them surging ahead could mean surgery—for me, tangled in two leashes. Then there is barking. Io is a very intelligent dog, she learns quickly. God forbid a pin should drop at four A.M. three floors below my apartment. On such an occasion, although not as rare as you might suppose, pin-dropping being what it is, Dog 1 will growl knowingly, then Dog 2 will bark I told you so. By four-oh-two, Dog 1 is barking at Dog 2 to shut up. Or is that me?

My girls. They whine when I leave, they pee on the rug the moment I return.

They'll play with each other. That's what the pediatrician said to my mother after she missed her period two months after my delivery. What he left out is the part about fighting. My sister reminds me of the crayon line drawn down the middle of our double bed, how I threatened her with slaughter if any of her limbs dared cross it. I can't throw a ball to the dogs without starting a fight. They wrestle and growl and literally put their jaws around each other's throats but there's been no blood so far, although fur has flown. I've been told they'd be too exhausted to fight if they ran free for hours. I am sure that if my sister and I had separate bedrooms we would have gotten along fine too. So I ameliorate, facilitate, negotiate. Two dogs turn out to be not two times one. I give them two nice bones and one has to keep both from the other. Didn't I spend every waking hour hoarding my own bones for some eighteen years?

They do eat from the same bowl. They do lick each other's ears, albeit mostly after plunging their snouts into the ice cream tub. They do sleep curled together. They also hump each other, a big advantage in having a serious dog friend. But it's like heavy petting—they don't give a big heave and fall exhausted to the floor but keep it up, keep it up. I suppose it beats working over the legs of visitors the way certain boy dogs do. This grand lesbian love is usually played out mornings, one girl melding into the other as a bouncing headdress, flouting it. At least Mom never had to lose any sleep over that one.

Dealing with double dog makes me think Mom and I are two different breeds. After all, for a long time I thought I was adopted, that I had North Shore Animal Shelter written all over me. It was her dark skin, dark eyes, quick comebacks to my light everything, my ponderous two-day-old retorts. I'm sure if we barked she would be low and sulky and I would yap at the mailman's heels. Playing Mom with the two of them makes me appreciate our differences in style. After all, Spot will snap and eat flies until her jaws ache—and Io's never the least bit tempted.

But playing Mom breaks down to doing what you know. Myself and my siblings responded to psychology, thank you very much. Bait and switch, Pavlovian behaviorism (we could salivate better than any Russian dog), deprivation, and just plain punishment. I'd like not to do that but instinctively—people have instincts too—I slip. I find myself praising Io to lure Spot back in line and instantly hear my mother's *Good girl* to my sister's scales while I shirked practice. But where do I get the idea that I am in charge anyway, that alpha dog concept? From a book, like my own mother, with Spock. I'm really just a procurer for the dogs, somebody with a talent for creating leftovers. Mom says it's true, your only true power as a mother is in meal planning. Then I meet Moses. A friend's perfectly normal-looking beagle, the dog opens his own cans with his teeth and then eats the can too (true! true!). A dog who feeds himself! Forget all about anything alpha, I'm only in charge of Good dog, Bad dog.

But I still need help, now more than ever. Mom—I plead for advice—what about the dogs' atrocious street manners? She suggests I dip a pizza crust in alum so the dogs won't ever want to hoover the sidewalks for trash again. (You should have seen those dogs pucker up!) It is a great revelation to think my mother knows anything about animals, let alone dogs. When I was growing up, the closest our family came to having a pet—other than whoever was youngest—was a plague of ladybugs in the garage every October. Has Mom been reading up? Talking to a neighbor for counsel? Is there a side of her I don't guess, a side that isn't Mom but someone else, someone who lives in the world without me? A real person?

Right after Spot's adoption, she told me I was crazy to take on so much responsibility. Like I couldn't handle it, given my revolving-door policy with the males of my own species. Dogs heel, I told her, and they don't make you cry in the middle of the night. Besides, I said, presenting my trump card, it's a girl, she won't mark your furniture. Do you have any rugs? she asked. When I brought Io around for her blessing, she threw up her hands. With shedding like that, she said, you could open a sweater factory.

I thought she'd never come around. Last year she did keep Spot an extra day after I came back from vacation—only so Spot could finish off an old pot roast, you understand. I also noticed she couldn't stop exclaiming over how Io picks up my loose socks, the one trick she remembers from all that training. Could dogs bring us together? Just last week she confesses she's been eyeing a Rhodesian Ridgeback in a pet store window. "You turned out all right," she said. "I think I'll name it after you."

HOW
TO BE
ALONE

Ken Foster

Some days, in the dog run a few blocks from my apartment, I watch my dog Brando from a distance and see him suddenly withdraw from a game with his dog friends, scanning the benches that border the run, trying to remain cool while craning his neck, looking for me. I wait quietly at first, and then I give in. "Over here!" I yell, and he races over to tag me with his nose, and then runs back again to rejoin the game. He likes to keep track of his people.

During the first months he lived with me, I opened my eyes during the night and found him sitting next to my head, staring down at me, as if I was a subject he was studying; when he realized he had been discovered, he would move silently to the bottom of the bed, curl up, and close his eyes, pretending that nothing had taken place while I was sleeping, nothing at all. If the quilt sometimes formed a mountain that hid my face from his view, Brando couldn't trust that I remained just a few feet away from him and would creep closer to peer cautiously over the temporary barricade that had come between us.

Sometimes, I pretended to be asleep as he licked my entire head, carefully, while I waited, testing him to see how far he would go. Once, I woke to find him arranged with our nostrils aligned, his breathing synchronized so that the same air passed back and forth between us. At this point I decided that perhaps he'd gone a little too far.

Dogs are pack animals; their existence and behavior are built on establishing and maintaining their position in a group. It's for this reason that many people find dogs annoying. We tend to be far less social as a species, when it really comes down to it, than we might like to think. For humans, social activity has become something we choose, or something we resist. For dogs, interacting is an irresistible impulse and for some dogs, like Brando, every time a person walks away from them it triggers a sense of panic at the possibility of losing part of the pack.

It was on an illegal trip to Havana, Cuba, that I realized I had gone dog crazy. There I was surrounded by mojitos and jazz musicians, military soldiers on every corner, a suspicious stamp in the back of my passport, and what struck me most was the absence of dogs. Where had they gone? Even the strays were rare, and suggested to me the reason for their absence: In a country with so little food, there wasn't anything left to give them.

If I had traveled there a few months earlier, I wouldn't have noticed this at all. In Manhattan, I'd always been one of the people who didn't "get" dogs and sneered at the legions of people who opened their tiny apartments to these things and allowed their schedules to be ruled by them. What was the appeal? How could anyone be charmed by a creature so nakedly manipulative, so demanding of our time?

But I'd been living in Costa Rica and I'd fallen in love there with a dog. Duque came to my apartment each night and took his place on a chair next to the door. During the day he would guide me around the edges of the property, showing me trails along the hills that even the farm's inhabitants had forgotten. Sometimes he would stop over a particular view and look up at me, to make sure that I was seeing it too: the bright flowers growing on the other side of a ravine. He ignored the leisurely retirees in the neighboring houses and sometimes he ignored me, but he always followed the gardener and housekeeper on their daily chores, fascinated by every boring task they were expected to complete. In the villages and on the beaches were mismatched packs of dogs, living the high life, swimming in the surf, flirting with the tourists, better behaved than any leashed dog in the city.

"You've lost your mind," my mother told me, each time I e-mailed her about Duque. "You must be lonely. You have no one to talk to." It was true, I didn't speak the language. But I didn't speak dog either, and that hadn't stopped him from finding a way of approaching me. Meanwhile, my hosts were a little absent, bored with the idea of having a guest (and who could blame them: I'd been staying there for months). They'd grown too accustomed to living there to show me what was unique.

Duque roamed most of the time, splitting his time between me and the gardener, between the farm and a little road in the village where José Luis and his entire extended family lived in a series of houses. He was fed once a day, when Cecilia, the cook, put whatever was left over from lunch into his bowl: chicken bones, beans, rice, peppers, avocado. Once, I passed his dish and saw that just a single slice of toast had been left for him.

In the evenings, when everyone was gone, I began to include him in my meals. The truth is, I cooked for him. I'm not sure what I would have prepared if I'd just been cooking for one, but with a dog to feed I shopped with care, cooking fish or chicken with brown rice, and splitting it between us. Then we would retire to my studio and sleep through till the morning, Duque getting up occasionally to patrol the grounds. The night before my trip to Cuba, he sat on his chair pretending to be sleeping, watching me pack through his not-quite-closed eyes. In the morning he stood with me on the porch, sitting patiently while I loaded the taxi, and though usually he followed me whenever I left him, this time he stayed there, and watched as the car pulled away.

When I announced, at the end of December, that'd I'd be taking the dog with me to New York, suddenly even the most distracted members of the farm felt the need to address me. "You don't understand the dogs here," one said. "You want them to be treated like children." No, I insisted, I just want him to be treated like a dog. But the people in the town knew him, and the gardener needed to say only one thing to me. It didn't require words. José Luis simply walked up to me and shook his head, and I knew I would be leaving without Duque.

Returning from the jungle to a winter in New York City was jarring to say the least. I'd been out of town for six months. I didn't remember what it was I'd done with my time. And more than anything, I missed that dog, missed his snoring in the corner of the room. In e-mailed reports, I heard he was now living like a hobo, disappearing for days at a time before returning again. If I was going to be spending my time worrying about a dog, I thought it ought to be one who was actually living with me.

I found Brando on the Internet, after finding my way to a Web site called Petfinder, where you can search shelters across the country by breed, size, gender, and age. I remember filling in the search form, thinking I could find a match for Duque, the one I was missing. Mixed, small, male, young. A list of choices appeared, each with a small photo, none of which looked anything like Duque. By the time I had crossed the river to Brooklyn, I'd decided getting a dog was an awful idea, but I went to the shelter to look anyway, since I was there. I walked into the place, a windowless room of barking dogs, and was doubly sure that I'd be better off living alone. Then I turned and saw him, a skinny copper-brown- and black-striped sock-puppet of a dog, staring quietly up at me. I knew it was him.

I decided that it would be best for both of us— Brando and me—to make this transition slowly. I arranged to visit him every morning for a week, while in the afternoon I shopped for dog dishes and toys and things, transforming my tiny studio apartment into a puppy nursery. I bought books about training dogs and establishing boundaries and, most important, teaching the dog how to be alone.

I took the L train each morning over to Brooklyn and walked through the snow to the shelter, where Brando would race out of his pen to greet me, doing a quick spin around the room to rub it in the noses of the other dogs. He had a person, and they didn't.

But once we got outside, he wouldn't go any-where. He planted himself on the sidewalk in front of the shelter, refusing to move. I sat with him, or carried him to a park nearby where he played but never with the enthusiasm he showed when we returned to the shelter and he ran back into his little fenced-in booth. He wouldn't even go to the bathroom outside, always waiting until we had returned and then going in his pen. It was as if he didn't want to give up any of the few things he knew were his. Once, I walked him toward the shopping area several blocks away, hoping the activity would interest him. But when we had gotten that far, he sat down again, and I sat with him, and the shoppers smiled awkwardly at the two of us as they passed, thinking we were homeless.

Before the week was up, I couldn't take leaving him behind anymore. On Sunday morning I turned the corner to see Brando out on the street in front of the shelter, about to go on a walk with a volunteer dog walker. Brando looked up and, seeing me in the distance, took a few steps away from the walker, keeping his eyes on me until I ran up and announced, "That's my dog. I'll take him." They called a car service from inside, and Brando sat in the back with me, licking my face the entire way back to Manhattan.

Brando had been found wandering the streets on December 27, but whoever had left him out hadn't thought to remove his vaccination tag, so the shelter was able to trace some of his history. His first owner had returned to Puerto Rico unexpectedly and left the dog behind "temporarily" with a friend, who claimed he had run away. But it's hard to see how a dog in the city can run away from home, and it seemed more likely that the second owner had holiday plans that a foster dog didn't fit into. On the records they gave me with his adoption, under NAME it read *Nene*—baby—and then, above it, *File under Brando*. Someone had decided he needed a new name.

I tried to imagine who would name a dog Baby and then so easily leave him behind.

Another reason getting a dog seemed like a fine, logical choice was my total lack of employment. Surely it would take months before I found a job, and so we would have those weeks together to settle things between us. Just as I was deciding on Brando, though, I found a couple of months of freelance work doing research in Midtown. But this is even better, I thought. This will establish immediately that he can't expect me to always be around.

All of the books I had read before "the adoption" had encouraged the use of a "crate" or cage to contain the dog in the owner's absence, to encourage house-training and keep the dog from chewing on things—varnished furniture, electrical wires, shoes—that might harm him if not irritate you upon your return. Dogs are den animals, they said. By keeping him in a locked crate, they said, I would be encouraging his own soothing instincts for safety.

Brando felt differently. Once I had lured him into the crate with a treat and closed the door, he would grip the metal grid door in his mouth, shaking it like a scene from a prison movie. He emitted sounds that resembled a variety of exotic tropical birds. Neighbors commented on it—not just the noise itself, but the fact that it sounded like a bird. In a matter of days he became suspicious of the whole thing, never stepping into the crate without first pushing the door open and closed several times with his nose to make sure it was working. Once he was inside, I would latch it on him again, just as I had done the day before.

I never worked more than four hours, because I worried that something would happen, and I wanted to spend time with him. After all, wasn't that the point of having a dog? To spend time with him? Each afternoon when I returned and opened the crate, Brando tumbled out onto the floor at my feet, honking like a clown horn before jumping onto my bed, the stage on which he proceeded to perform an elaborate can-can dedicated to me, kicking his greyhoundish legs in the air. Then, as if concerned that he might somehow lose the attention he'd been waiting for all day, he began nipping at my hands, until one night I shut myself in the bathroom to get away from him. And then, he began to cry.

A week later, I arrived home to find him waiting for me just inside the door. He wagged his tail and brushed up against me, as if looking to be rewarded for his accomplishment: He'd gotten out of the crate on his own. It took a minute for this to register, and then I ran over to check the door, which was ajar, but bewilderingly, the latch was still in the closed position. Scattered around the room were various items that he'd gotten into: a bag of treats, some clothes, a pile of poop, a puddle of pee, and several disposable razors he had taken from the bathroom. As I picked up the razors, which were in pieces, I realized that there was one piece of each that was missing: The triple blades were gone. He had eaten them.

When I was three, I'd once stuffed a little wooden man up my nose while my parents were attending a party up the street, and they had to return with a doctor to get it out. I'd also had a habit of getting myself out of my own crib when I was even younger, so much so that when at two I had broken my leg, it was only when I didn't climb out of my crib that my parents knew something was wrong. Now it was all coming around again.

"Feed him bread," the vet told me. "Believe it or not the razors will pass." Not satisfied, I dismantled another razor and saw that the blades were so thin, I was able to tear them with my hands. When I left the next day, I locked the bathroom door, in case he might escape again. And he did. He was going through a new segment of the apartment each day, taking inventory of things he'd been watching me use while we were together. This time it was the things piled on the chair next to the door, and my luggage, where he found more razors and ate them.

Just having me there wasn't enough. If I sat on the bed, hunched over my laptop, trying to get to work on something new of my own, Brando would arrange himself just behind the screen, where he could stare at me, incredulous at my insistence that anything short of him might be worthy of my focus. When staring didn't work, he joined me at the keyboard, pressing SEND on dozens of e-mail messages before I'd actually finished writing them. Finally, he settled in behind me, where I could use him as backrest or pillow.

Although I hadn't thought of it in a long time, I'd known another dog like Brando, so consistently on the verge of self-destructive hysteria. I was in college,

living in a house off campus, and one of the other
guys in the house brought home a stray without asking anyone else's permission. He was gone in classes all
day and worked all night, so he was rarely home to
take care of the dog. His own room was too small for
the dog to stay in, so he was kept in the kitchen,
where he cried all day and jumped desperately onto
anyone going in or out of the house. Whenever he
could, the dog squeezed out the door to run around
the neighborhood looking for his new and absent
master. The rest of us never bothered to go out looking when he was missing. In arguments with this
housemate, he always painted the rest of us as being
selfish for not accepting his dog. One day, a man came
to the door asking about the dog. Yes, we admitted, he
did live there. "I've got his head in my car," he said.
The man had struck him with his car, and when he
got out to check on the dog, it nipped him, so he took
off the head to be tested for rabies.

When I talked to the vet about Brando's problem
being alone, he said, "But you've only had him a few
weeks." It seemed unlikely to him that we would have
acquired such a strong bond so quickly. When I called
the people who had sold me the crate and told them
he'd escaped, they said, "That's not possible." When I
called a therapist, or behaviorist as they are called in the

animal world, she asked, "You don't coddle him, do you?" He was next to me of course, his head in my lap, his little body serving as an armrest.

"Coddle him?" I asked. "Isn't that the whole point?"

Brando wasn't Duque, and Manhattan wasn't the jungle, but still I thought he'd be good for me: the responsibility, the need to keep a schedule. There was a difference between a dog who chooses to visit you and one you choose to take home. Now, with two suicide attempts in as many days, my feelings had turned around completely. He had acted out for my attention, and rather than seeing it for what it was, I fell into a neurotic, fierce, protective love for him.

"You need to ignore him when you are home," the behavior therapist told me, a difficult task in a one-room apartment. "And when you are gone, you need to enroll him in day care."

What they don't tell you is that it is contagious; once you realize what the dog is capable of doing with-out you, you find yourself unable to ever leave him alone again. Even after the extravagance of enrolling him in a day-care program, I felt inadequate, a failure, the way I imagine some women feel when they leave their new baby for the first time to return to work.

Other people could manage it, leaving their dog for the day, remaining productive and worry-free, returning to their apartment without incident. Where had I gone wrong? And if he got into trouble at day care, a fight with another dog or, worse, with one of the humans, could they ever be as understanding as I might be? After signing all the papers the first day, I sat in the office with the day-care staff, mortified at the sudden sensation that I might cry. I was leaving him there for just four hours.

In spite of me, Brando began to feel a little too comfortable at day care. Like a child starting out at a new school, Brando cultivated a reputation as a troublemaker, roughhousing among the other dogs while simultaneously charming the staff. He liked to sit with them in the office when the other dogs were gone at the end of the day. He impressed them with acts of charity. There was an old lame dog who was kept in a bed in a room away from all of the action. "Brando likes to visit with him in the afternoon," one girl told me. "He's so sweet!"

This same girl became my first rival for his affection. She was Latin, with long black hair that she sometimes let Brando pull while he sat in her lap in the office. When I arrived to pick him up, Brando would run down the hall to me and leap into my arms, but by the time we collected his things and headed for the elevator he'd be reluctant to leave, thinking perhaps that we should just move in there with everyone else, since it was so much bigger than our apartment. He would sit, stubbornly refusing to enter the elevator, or, even more painful to witness, he would run back and forth between the staff and me, unable to decide to whom he should be loyal.

When my assignment ended, I was thrilled with the idea that I could get my dog back full time. I weaned him off day care, but for months, whenever he saw a woman with long black hair in the distance, he squealed and raced to catch up to her. "It's not her," I would tell him as he dragged me by the leash. Eventually, he gave up looking.

Not much is known for sure about what makes separation anxiety strike some dogs and not others. It is more likely in neutered animals, in animals with single owners, in animals who have been abandoned, but not animals who have been passed among multiple owners. It is unheard of in Europe, which doesn't surprise me at all, because in Europe you can also bring your dog with you nearly everywhere. Brando qualifies on every level, with bonus points, I imagine, for living in Manhattan.

In the past year, Brando has grown from a delicate-looking whippet-shaped dog to something more like a greyhound-mastiff-Great Dane—the mix changes as he continues to get bigger. He has destroyed four metal cages, including one billed as "Gorilla-Tough." He's scratched his face by forcing it through the bars; he's scraped the enamel from his teeth. It isn't the cage itself he minds, because when I am home, he'll spend time in it without complaint, just as he doesn't cry when I am present, or even if I am outside the door, within earshot. When he manages to get out of the crate, anything goes. I return to find a metal can impaled on his teeth, a newspaper slipped into the door frame by a neighbor to muffle the noise of my dog pounding to get out of the apartment. Once, I left him in the cage in front of the TV during an address by the president and returned to find the cage filled halfway with shredded copies of *The New York Times,* the television unplugged, the cord pulled into the cage and buried beneath the *Times.*

Dogs believe in family the way the Ticos in Costa Rica do, which may be why the two seem to me so inseparable. Big extended families, all living in the same building or along the same street, never splitting up or moving very far away: This is what dogs expect from us. In Ciudad Colón, when I walked to the village to get a bus that would take me into the city, Cecilia, the cook, would scrunch up her nose as I passed. "Why would anyone want to go there?" Duque agreed, following me to the stop and waiting with me, then staring through the window at me as the bus pulled away.

Imagine a dog's confusion assimilating into the North American family, where children and grand-parents are shipped off at the earliest convenience, leaving empty rooms to be remodeled or used as storage. My own parents, like so many others of their generation, waited until the children were gone before expanding the size of their house, so that the two of them could have more room to spread out in. After the renovations, I found real and imagined excuses for not coming home for a visit, meeting my parents in hotel rooms in other cities rather than returning to the transformed house I grew up in.

When I adopted Brando, my parents were as mortified as if I'd become a single parent. They argued with me, they rationalized. I wouldn't want the responsibility, they said. I wouldn't be able to travel. When I answered that it was time for me to stop traveling, that a little responsibility might be something good, they came up with a final ultimatum: I would never be allowed to visit them with the dog.

Six weeks later they drove to the city in their white van to pick us up for Brando's first vacation in the country. He was cautious at first, settling into the very back of the van, where they had laid out a dog bed for him, but soon he moved into my lap and then, realizing who was really in charge, he settled between my parents' bucket seats for the rest of the four-hour drive.

Most, if not all, of Brando's experience indoors consisted of my small apartment, where we did little other than write and sleep, and the large day-care center, where he was allowed to run up and down the long hallway, playing as hard as he liked. My parents' house is a T-shaped ranch house, with each room opening into the next and a group of bedrooms clustered at one end. To keep him out of the fancier areas, including the extension, a crate blocked the way from the kitchen to the living and dining area, and the door in an adjoining study and subsequent hall was kept closed. Nothing could be more infuriating to Brando. It was bad enough that there was all this space within his sight, but beyond his range. What made it even worse was our insistence on entering and exiting in every direction: into the bathrooms, into the hall, into the basement and the garage. He could never keep all of the family together in one room, and whoever was missing, he waited at the door closest to the direction they had left in, his nose pressed against the crack at the base of the door frame, sniffing for signs of their return.

In the morning on our visits there, Brando wakes up early and goes out to the kitchen, his tail wagging in anticipation until my mother comes out in her robe to start the coffee. When my father arrives, Brando begins his dancing, his hips swiveling like Elvis, or a frantic hula dancer in a grass skirt. What makes it thrilling to him is the boring sameness of the fact that the four of us are together again in the same place, at the same time, just like the day before. Then after coffee comes the shocker, we will all be going in different directions, he hasn't managed to convince us to stay, just as he hasn't managed to convince us at bedtime to sleep all together in one bed.

For Brando, my father is the worst offender, often retreating after dinner into the extension, sliding the doors closed, and sitting alone watching television. This makes no sense to Brando, since my mother and I are watching TV too, in the family room, where Brando is allowed to lounge on the floor in a carefully calculated spot between us. What could the point be in doing anything on your own?

Because of the shape of the house, and the large windows facing into the backyard and woods at the edge of the property, Brando often leads me back to a spot where he can stand and peer out the window, across the patio, and in through the windows on the other side, where the shadow of my father is visible, sitting alone, reading or watching television.

We can stand that way—together—for quite a while, staring at the distance.

THE DOG
GUILT TRIP—
A TRAVELOGUE

Nicholas Dawidoff

I was into my thirties before I got my first puppy, and people who know me would say that right from day one, I got exactly what I was asking for. Standing there in a Virginia barn, waiting for my new yellow Lab/standard poodle mix pup to be taken from the litter and brought out to me, I already loved my Maybelle and couldn't do enough for her. And then, when small, white-blond, fluffy young Maybelle appeared, her feelings for me were just as clear. She made an ecstatic leap into my arms and peed all over me.

As a bright-eyed native Virginian who tends to keep on the sunny side, Maybelle is in many ways a credit to her namesake, Mother Maybelle Carter, of the musical Carter Family. It is also true that Maybelle plays me like a five-string guitar. I am a first-class traveler on the dog guilt trip; a flagrant apologist for my bad little dog.

Now, Maybelle and I are not as disgraceful in this respect as some dogs and owners I know. (There I go again.) A few months back I ran into a friend and noticed how trim he was. "You've lost weight," said I. "You are looking terrific."

"It's the new dog," he explained. "She gets all the credit."

"I know what you mean. Forces you to get out there and get exercise even on rainy days or when you are tired. It's so great."

"No, no," he said. "It's mostly that I'm just eating less. I feel bad eating in front of her. You know, sitting there gobbling up things she can't have. Like pasta puttanesca. And chocolate cake. So I don't. I mean, I still eat, and all. But much less."

With Maybelle, things quickly went awry. On her second weekend in New York, we visited some friends for the Super Bowl and I insisted on bringing her along. My friend's children would, of course, want to see the new puppy, and this way we'd also be able to walk her at halftime. To this point I had never heard Maybelle bark. In the first quarter she began to make up for lost time. It was a pitched, ringing, strident sound—a genuine yap. My friend's father, a big football fan with blood pressure problems, looked uneasy. "She's just excited," I volunteered. "Big game. New experiences. She'll settle down and go to sleep soon." I took her outside for a stroll. Early in the third quarter, my friend's father's team was losing. Perhaps he had a wager on the game. Adding to his troubles was the young dog barking insistently at his gouty ankle and giving it the occasional gnaw. I was encouraged to put her in the laundry room, which I did. She barked for a while and then quieted down.

What they tell you about dog's tails telling the tale is all true. When Maybelle was sprung from the laundry room, she exited tail between her legs, eyes downcast, head shifting from side to side. There was poop all over the walls.

"That's what we get for sticking her in there and locking her up when she's just a baby," I said to my wife on the way home. This was also my rejoinder when we dropped off Maybelle with some other friends for a day while we were out of town. They left her alone for a while. Whereupon our perfectly toilet-trained dog peed right in the middle of their bed.

"That dog cannot expect to be with someone every living minute," my wife would say after each transgression, but Maybelle did expect that, and worked hard at achieving her aim. I'd take her to the post office, tie her up outside, and—bedlam. I'd go away for a couple of hours, come home and find ravaged shoes and old keepsakes chewed to atoms.

Maybelle specialized in devouring sentiment. My 1933 Moe Berg baseball card was pulped. I placed things even higher out of reach, but it did no good. Maybelle, it seems, is a top-shelf climber. A particularly treasured note from my sister was shredded. Maybelle even dipped into my wife's first letters to me. "She's teething," I'd say to my wife. "She gets lonely. All those hours by herself. I only wish she could read, or was interested in Egyptian art or classical music. What else is there for her to do all day but get into a little trouble. She's obviously bored."

"You," said my wife, "are obviously a lunatic."

Particularly insidious was that Maybelle would punctuate her destructive episodes with just enough angelic goodwill that we didn't put her into a box and ship her back to Virginia. Sometimes it was a near thing. She learned her commands very quickly and could perform them like a West Point cadet, particularly when there was food on the line.

But if the incentive wasn't so alluring, she became disinclined. That is to say that she tugged mercilessly on her leash everywhere I took her. "She's not pulling," I'd tell my wife, my arm half out of its socket. "She just thinks we're running." Another day I wanted to know how it could be that a dog knew fifteen commands after five days, but could never learn "heel." Not long after that, my wife refused to walk with me and the dog.

My wife is a sweet-natured soul, but she is also firm. Further, she knows animals. She grew up raising animals on a farm and believes in discipline. At a certain point, I received an ultimatum. Either I took the dog to an obedience school or she didn't know what.

There are few more humbling experiences than coming to terms with the fact that your dog is the dunce of the class and it's all your fault. Each week,

Maybelle and I reported to a basement-level room in a local pet shop, where Maybelle joyfully pounced on her new playmates. When it came time for the session to begin, she continued pouncing so that other owners were soon referring to her as "that dog," and "that Maybelle," as in "let's keep Harry away from that Maybelle so we can get something done in here." Some owners thought getting their dog to ignore Maybelle was part of the curriculum. One real class exercise involved instructing your dog to sit and stay while you walked to the far end of the shop, and called your dog. Soon enough, all the other dogs came dutifully on command. Maybelle, on the other hand, always went straight for the tropical fish. I couldn't really blame her. I come from a long line of seafood lovers.

Each week in the class I was given a great deal of instruction about consistency and firmness. I was also told, in passing, that I owned "a willful, high-strung dog." Each time afterward, I would arrive home demoralized. My wife would ask how it went. From my horizontal perch along an armchair I would mumble about "being humiliated" by "our *very* willful, high-strung dog." My wife would want details. "I can't remember them anymore," I'd say. "She was a wild blur in there and now my memory is blurred." My wife would want to know what the teacher had to say about this. "I think she thinks I'm doing an outstanding job under the circumstances," I'd reply. "She says Maybelle can't help it. Maybelle is an *unusually* willful and high-strung dog." To this my wife would say "oh."

The last week of the class was reserved for the grand finale—an obedience exam. The dogs would have to perform a series of commands under the observation of three judges. People in the class were bringing friends and family to watch the triumphs of little Harry and good little Tyler. In the days leading up to this event, I sunk into a malaise. Finally one evening I hit bottom and turned to my wife. "Sweetie," I said. "Is Maybelle going to flunk?" I was fixed with a look. "I think," my wife said, "that in your mind you are convinced Maybelle is a good dog." I began to protest. My wife continued in a tone that did not brook further interruption. "When Maybelle runs wind sprints through the bedroom at two in the morning, you don't say 'No.' You look aggrieved for her and say 'She didn't get enough exercise today.' When Maybelle licks a guest's shoes, you say 'She only wants to participate and this is how dogs participate.' When she leaps onto the table and eats your grandmother's hamburger right off her plate, Maybelle is 'just hungry.' C'mon, honey. Somehow you don't see her for what she is."

"Will you take her to the exam?" I asked. But my wife was already asleep.

The day of the obedience test Maybelle and I walked over to the pet store. In the schoolroom the other owners were putting their dogs through their last practice paces. Maybelle was trying to strike up conversations. At a certain point I was slumped in a corner massaging my dog-walking shoulder, Maybelle was chewing happily through her sixteenth leash, and then came a fresh breeze across my brow. "Maybelle," said my wife. "Drop." The leash went to the floor.

Eleven dogs were on hand for the test. Maybelle, seeded last, would be eleventh to go. She sat quietly on one side of my wife while I remained on the other. Then, at last, it was Maybelle's turn. "C'mon Maybelle!" I shouted. "You can do it pup." Maybelle barked and pawed at my chest. My wife glared at me. "You," she said, "will stand behind the door and watch through the window in a way that this dog cannot see you."

From where I peered, the whole thing really was something to behold. When my wife said "sit" Maybelle fell to her seat like an apple from the tree. She plummeted to "down," came with a shot zooming right past the fish tanks, became a statue at "stay," and, for good measure, shook paws like a debutante and sat pretty in a way that would have made a prairie dog proud. The judges were astonished and most impressed. "Good job," they scribbled on her score sheet. To my wife they said a lot of other uplifting things about never counting any dog out.

On the way home we were all looking very pleased with ourselves. My wife diverted me from buying Maybelle a victory ice cream cone—"people food"—but I did get to gloat. At least for a while. It was about at the point where I was claiming that clearly the school was "a cat-gone rip-off" because "Maybelle could do it better than any of them all the time, especially that fop cur Harry" that my wife said, "I think I am going to tear up this diploma and save Maybelle the trouble."

"You can't do that," I said. "It's mine." There was no response. Traffic quieted. A cloud passed in front of the sun. The streetlight changed and changed again. There are not many Eureka moments in life, and this was one for me. "Give me that leash," I said. My wife handed it over. "Listen, you worthless dog," I said. "If you are not good, I am not good, and that is not good. Do we understand each other?"

Since then I have been receiving many compliments on my "new tone with the dog," and my "elegant mix of authority and affection." There are people who think that before long, I might even be ready for children.

New York
Is for the
Dogs

Hillary Rosner

George is sitting in the window, barking. This is true as I write this, and it is most likely true as you read this. As sure as tomorrow will come, if there's a window to sit by and people to bark at, George will be doing just that.

We live on the second floor, so from his perch in the faded pumpkin wing chair that's nestled right up against the windowsill, he could almost reach out and lick the top of someone's head with his long drooly tongue. There's no shortage of heads to choose from, either. We live on a busy street in Greenwich Village, and day and night the pedestrians flow past George's perch, gabbing, shouting, sometimes even singing. George barks at most of them, but especially at their dogs. When a dog trots by, George will leap to his feet—still in the chair—and pounce at the window, his toenails scratching the paint off the radiator as he bounces up and down, seventy pounds of muscley canine, leaving chips of white paint and plaster in tell-tale piles on the floor.

Peso watches with amusement, her graying muzzle quivering slightly whenever George lets fly an especially loud howl. Not so long ago, she would sometimes jump into the chair herself and growl at passing dogs. But since George's arrival three months ago, Peso has settled contentedly into the role of older sister. She wrestles him to the ground, lets him take her whole solid neck between his vampire fangs, stands dutifully still while he licks her right ear with monomaniacal enthusiasm—but when his childish exuberance leads him to jump up and down on the windowsill, her beautiful almond-shaped eyes twinkle with unmistakable wonder that anyone could be so young and so easily entertained.

So it goes in my two-dog New York City world. I work from home, so Peso and George and I spend our days together. Nights when my boyfriend returns from the office, we all wrestle around for a while before getting on to whatever social engagements we (the two-legged creatures) have planned. Last thing before bed, first thing in the morning, and several times in between, we walk the dogs. Every time I turn around, someone needs to go out, or is waiting to get fed, or has just thrown up and needs to be tended to. I have friends who only go home to sleep—they jet from office to gym to dinner to drinks, and on weekends spend all day at museums and galleries and movies. I am rarely away from home for more than five hours.

There are toys and food to be bought, behavioral problems (barking, for instance) to address, veterinarians to consult. And I'm not just talking about stocking up on Purina and taking them for annual vaccinations.

Most dog food is made from whatever's left over after the choice parts of the meat are used for human consumption; some foods even contain ash from dogs that were euthanized at the pound. Not for my dogs, thank you: Peso and George eat organic food called Solid Gold. Unfortunately (and unrelated to the food), Peso has had more than her share of medical problems: cruciate ligament surgery on both knees (fifteen hundred dollars a pop, though pet insurance covered half), half a dozen little tumors and cysts removed (all, thankfully, benign), and, in the downtime, an impressive assortment of rashes.

My human friends and relatives have resigned themselves to my obsessive dog-love, so when my cousins call from down South you can be sure they'll remember to ask after George and Peso even before I ask about their kids. I'm amassing an impressive (or worrisome) collection of dog-inspired gifts: a kitschy ceramic ashtray ringed by sculpted boxer puppy cigarette rests; an iron-on dalmatian patch; a T-shirt silkscreened with a photograph of Peso. My photographer sister has been dutifully documenting my dog days since the first months with Peso, so my apartment walls are hung with framed prints, lest anyone fail to appreciate the depth of my devotion.

People think I'm crazy. I invariably mention one

of the dogs when I'm talking to someone new (the way one might unconsciously use the pronoun *we* instead of *I,* except in my case *we* sometimes means me and the dogs), which leads them to ask, "Oh, you have a dog? What kind?"

"Actually, I've got two," I reply. They picture dachshunds, Jack Russell terriers, perhaps a couple of pugs. "One is a boxer and the other is a dalmatian mix—possibly part Great Dane."

They try to visualize it. Maybe they picture their own itty-bitty space, imagine themselves tripping over massive beasts every time they try to use the toilet or squeeze into the closet-sized kitchen. They search their memories for some buried detail of my financial picture: Do I have a trust fund? A Hollywood contract? A relative in real estate? Finally they ask, "How big is your apartment?"

"It's a one-bedroom," I tell them. "Relatively large, as far as they go. But just a one-bedroom." The apartment is eight hundred square feet, big by Manhattan standards. Sometimes I reveal this superfluous information and sometimes I leave it out; occasionally I'll point out that even a studio half that size sure beats a cramped and lonely cage at an animal shelter. But usually I keep my mouth shut. They already have their suspicions about me.

"It must be a huge responsibility," they say. Which I understand to mean, *Are you nuts? Two large dogs in New York City? Why do you do it?*

They make me happy.

"But the hassle of cleaning up after them."

You get used to it.

"And the getting up early to walk them."

Sometimes we go back to bed afterward.

"And the difficulty of exercising them."

We go hiking a lot.

"Is it worth it?" they finally ask.

It's the only thing that makes life in New York tolerable.

I was born and raised on the Upper East Side. I went to elite private schools with classmates whose parents were rock stars, burning comets of Wall Street, supernovas of media galaxies. My own parents were cut more in the Horatio Alger mold, having pulled themselves up—from immigrant parents and poverty in Queens—to an upper-middle-class life where their children wanted for almost nothing. The one thing I always wanted but was never allowed was a dog. I wanted a dog so badly I would stand in the dog food aisle at the supermarket and look longingly at the lucky people

stacking their carts with cans of Alpo and those tanta-
lizing red boxes of Milk Bones. "It's cruel to keep a dog
in the city," my parents would say when I asked, several
times a year, why I couldn't have one. When I was old
enough to reply that it was crueler to put a dog down
at a shelter because no one came to adopt it, they
changed their rhetoric. "When you have your own
apartment, you can do whatever you want," went the
new line, which I repeated to myself all the way
through college.

The sum of my upbringing is supposed to be a
comfortable life as an urban professional: cocktail parties, openings, a country house in close proximity to
other people's country houses. For vacations I'm supposed to travel to European cities, perhaps to Southeast
Asia for a taste of the exotic. It turns out, however, that
I like to go to the woods. Don't get me wrong: I like
cocktail parties just fine. (I've tried to pretend that I
don't, but it's no use.) But I'd give them all up, honest,
for a cozy riverside cabin in some half-deserted western
town. Or a few years in a Costa Rican rain forest, waking up at dawn to macaws and howler monkeys, hiking
in the jungle a million miles from anywhere. I started
leaning this way after college, and began talking of plans
to move away, someplace with big sky. The reaction
from friends and family was as immediate as it was uni-

form: "It's a phase." "Oh please, you can't even go an hour without checking your e-mail," my friend Amanda says dismissively whenever I threaten to act on my pastoral yearnings. My mother tells me supportively, "Do what you need to do"; the subtext is *to get this silly thing out of your system,* presumably so I can start appreciating Carnegie Hall and the Metropolitan Museum instead of whining about the traffic.

It's true that I spent my childhood visiting art museums and the swank Park Avenue duplexes of friends like Olga of Greece. (Not just Olga *from* Greece, Olga *of* Greece. Like Charles *of* Wales.) Yes, I attended a middle school dance chaperoned by Mick Jagger and picked up junior high sex tips from Gwyneth Paltrow. In twelfth grade, we partied on weekends with a classmate—the son of an American magazine mogul—who had his own apartment across from the United Nations.

But surely it's no less important that my uncle, my father's brother, builds canoes in his garage in Madison, Wisconsin? For years he led canoe trips for the Sierra Club. Last summer, he spent two weeks paddling to the Arctic Ocean. In a recent photograph, he's out on a half-finished second-story porch with a power saw, his safety harness clipped to a hook on a tree branch. Two other plucky relatives on my father's side—great-uncles, I think—left Queens in the 1930s and shacked up in Alaska, panning for gold and racing dog sleds.

❖ ❖ ❖

I adopted Peso, my first dog, when I was twenty-four. I was living in a cavernous downmarket Soho loft with three roommates—a made-for-TV caricature of a twenty-something New York City lifestyle, complete with the groovy sitcom-style apartment that as a rule doesn't exist anywhere but on *Friends*. It bordered on ridiculous: Dylan was a rising player in the world of independent film; Drew was an aspiring documentary filmmaker who convinced a burgeoning Web development firm to fund his world travels in the name of marketing. Damion, my then-boyfriend, was pulling all-nighters at a multimedia start-up. I was working my way up the journalism food chain. There were parties, movie premiers, late-night dinners in trendy restaurants. But what really made me happy was to stay home and drink tea and go hiking on the weekends. I suppose in some way I viewed Peso as a litmus test. The idea was that I'd take her for walks in the woods, run with her on deserted beaches in winter, curl up by the fire with her in rented lakeside cabins. If all this felt right, if—to be corny about it—it brought me closer to inner peace, then I'd know my cosmopolitan persona was mainly a result of circumstance. I wanted to put nature versus nurture to the test, to see if this longing I felt to roam in wild places was in my blood and not just a symptom of some quarter-life crisis.

I found Peso through a local boxer rescue. Tough luck had landed her at the CACC, the city's bleak shelter, where tens of thousands of perfectly adoptable dogs are put down each year. She was in quarantine for mites. No one who came to pick out a pet would see her. She was scheduled to die in two days.

In a frantic effort to find her a home before time ran out, someone from the CACC had called someone from boxer rescue. We rushed to Brooklyn to see her; I was so nervous I could barely breathe. Was this going to be my dog? What if we stood face to face with each other and there was no connection? Could I possibly just leave this creature at the shelter, knowing I was the only thing that stood between her and lethal injection? Stuck in traffic, we arrived at the shelter just as the gates were closing. We ducked underneath and raced inside, where the woman to whom we'd spoken earlier was so happy to see us her eyes filled with tears. She brought Peso out to us, and there was this skinny little thing wiggling and wagging across the room as though she'd been waiting for me forever. We'd been forewarned about her condition: She was missing patches of fur on her neck, back, and feet from the mites. In my panic about actually getting a dog, though, I'd envisioned her looking far mangier than she did. Sure, she had a few bald spots, and her poor little nose was pink and scabbed at the tip from banging it against the bars of her cage. But she was utterly irresistible, her squishy face furrowed in expectation as she came toward us. She ran right up to me—me!—and gave me a kiss on the lips. And that was that.

I was thirty before I got my second dog, in a different apartment, a different relationship, a thousand experiences separating me from life in that Soho loft. *Mais plus ça change* . . . A friend who's known me since the seventh grade likes to say he marks his calendar by my escape fantasies. "Is it September already?" he laughs each year when I call to say I'm planning to leave New York.

But the strange thing about having Peso in my life was that as much as she confirmed my yearnings for a life outside the city, she also functioned as my personal self-help guru, teaching me to worship the small details. When we still lived in Soho, we'd sit on our small stoop for hours each day, me on the bottom step and Peso sprawled flat like a rug on the cool metal platform that stretched out toward the curb, with her wrinkly jowls spread flush around her face. When the wind shifted, she'd lift her head and sniff the air, and I'd sniff too, trying to smell what it was that had piqued her interest. New York is a city of intriguing odors—not to mention the people who leave them behind. We grew to know our neighbors on the block: the pot-smoking dealer in antique arcade games whose wife brokered deals on multimillion-dollar lofts; the forty-something couple whose avant-garde theater company was notorious for staging productions in the nude. Soho—before the artists were forced out by rising rents, replaced by high-end shops—was our Main Street.

And yet, and yet . . . Still I talked of fleeing, and still we remained. I took baby steps. I spent four summers teaching in Vermont, each spare moment passed frolicking with Peso in a river or lake or blissful mountainside. I considered accepting a job offer in San Francisco. I fell in love with a guy from New Mexico, who gets easily depressed by New York's concrete landscape and self-referential social hierarchies. Most recently, I downloaded applications for fellowships in Colorado and Michigan, and rented a house in Vermont for a few months.

But my emotional bond with New York is proving more tenacious than I'd realized. I am beginning to worry I'll never get out—that I'll be forty and still yammering on to whomever will listen about my big plans to flee to Montana. "This place is unhealthy," I fear I'll be saying six years on, just as I said it six years ago. "Too many people. Too little space. Too much aggression." Even Phil, my New Mexican boyfriend, quietly doubts my commitment to leaving the city. "You'll go crazy after a month," he warns.

I dreamed of getting another dog. There were so many thousands of them wasting away in shelters, sweet sad-eyed mutts who deserved a taste of the good life. Why not bring another one home? I also had other, selfish motivations. Getting the first dog had proved something to *me;* maybe a second would prove it to everyone else. "I'm the kind of person who has two dogs!" I could scream as I walked down Prince Street with leashes tangled in my hands, stooping to pick up two steaming piles of poop. "Surely I don't belong in this godforsaken town!" In truth, I'd wanted another dog for years, though there was a serious practical problem: Peso is an alpha bitch, and there are very few dogs she'll tolerate. I stopped taking her to the dog run early on in our days together, after it became a question not of whether she would start a fight, but how soon and with whom. (A friend even presciently named her little dog Snack in honor of Peso, who did in fact try to eat the Snack one fateful afternoon.) The handful of times another dog—even one she liked—crossed our threshold, Peso became a growling territorial monster. Though I certainly had my peaceful-doggie-brother-and-sister dreams, I was pretty sure Peso would never accept another canine in the family. At least not in New York. Too much aggression. Too little space.

In January, as a trial run, Phil and I agreed to house a rottweiler named Baker for a week from a no-kill rescue organization that had more dogs than it could handle. He was gorgeous, long and lean with overgrown paws and a tongue that always stuck slightly out, even when his mouth was closed. But Baker and Peso wanted to kill each other; Peso would snap viciously at Baker and he would respond by lunging at her, snarling, teeth bared. They'd go at each other for blood, and even pulling one dog off wouldn't help, since the other would just keep attacking. We sent Baker to stay with a friend temporarily, and eventually, after trying desperately for weeks on end to find him a home, we were forced to send him back to the shelter. We were heartbroken. The guilt, the feeling that we'd failed this poor dog, was unbearable.

In February (while Baker was still with the friend) we flew to Utah to volunteer at Best Friends, an animal sanctuary nestled in a canyon not far from Monument Valley. (Not quite Alaska, but vaguely in the right direction.) The country's largest sanctuary and a model of humane shelter care, it houses as many as eight hundred dogs at a time, living in big outdoor pens with individual doghouses filled with straw. Eight hundred dogs on a red clay plateau is an overwhelming spectacle. For three days we fed, walked, and cuddled them. One night we took a Doberman mix named Lanessa back to our cabin, to help the sanctuary assess her personality and hopefully improve her chances of getting adopted. I fell in love with her, and the next day fell again for an achingly handsome and soulful ten-year-old hound named Spud, who howled each time he saw me. His gaze tormented me, because I knew there was no way I could take him home. Logistics aside, there was a larger issue: Uprooting a backcountry dog to the city hardly seemed like rescue.

We first met George at New York's Union Square on a mild Saturday in early September: September 8, 2001. He'd been rescued from the CACC—the same shelter as Peso—by Mighty Mutts, the shelter that also housed Baker. I'd written an article about Mighty Mutts and its zany founder, who'd given up everything—including his wife—to rescue dogs and cats. Every Saturday, Mighty Mutts brings its charges to Union Square in the hope of finding homes. On an afternoon walk with Peso, we stopped by to say hello to a friend who was volunteering, and were soon surrounded by volunteers—who knew me from the article—egging us on to adopt another dog.

What ensued was much like what can happen when you walk into an expensive clothing store "just for fun" and quickly become caught up in the glamour of it all. (Not that this has ever happened to me, of course. Nature girls hate shopping.) You envision the life you will lead in a particular sweater or pair of pants before you remember that you had no intention of buying anything and besides, what good is a leopard-print mini in Colorado? There we were, Phil and I, taking various dogs in turn for a walk through the park with Peso, observing her reactions (alternately snarling and stoic), giggling like giddy teenagers at each pooch's goofy personality quirks. And then suddenly we landed back in reality. When we made good on our promise to move away, we told each other, then we'd be ready for another slobbering canine. But until then it would never work. We trudged back home to our still-calm, one-dog apartment.

But one Mighty Mutt—George—had gotten under my skin. I couldn't stop thinking about his big black ears that stuck straight out the side of his head like bat wings, and how he seemed to have charmed Peso into a state of complete disinterest on our test walk—which was as close to tolerance as I thought we'd ever get. Maybe we'd go back the next weekend and visit him again. Until then, though, there was work to do, deadlines, an Indian summer party to plan.

Three days later we awoke to a different world. We stood on Sullivan Street, a block from our apartment and just a mile north of the World Trade Center, and watched the towers burn. After the skyscrapers crumbled to ruins, we crept back home, shell-shocked, to check on Peso. Within minutes of stepping back outside to walk her, a bomb scare in a delivery truck sent hundreds of pedestrians—flowing up our street from Lower Manhattan—fleeing in panic. I held on tight to Peso's leash and kept her by my side all day.

My relationship to the city became even more complicated after September 11. If ever there was a time to flee, this seemed like it; yet I was torn between the desire to run away to someplace out of harm's way and the instinct to remain, to stand loyally with my city through dark times. I was afraid to stay—but almost as afraid to go. Would leaving make me a fair-weather friend?

The first few days after the attacks brought a pervasive civility to the city, its residents linked together in grief and shock. Strangers hugged each other and wept. The pace of life slowed down, as people wandered glassy-eyed through the streets of our neighborhood. When pedestrians bumped into each other, they stopped and apologized. In spite of the tragedy that had

stunned this new New York into being, it was a tanta-
lizing vision of the city's potential. I knew it couldn't
possibly last.

For several days no cars were allowed south of
14th Street, so we walked Peso through the quiet
downtown streets filled with people on skateboards and
bicycles. We tried not to keep her outdoors for too long
at a stretch, since the air was thick with the acrid smell
of smoke from the towers. When the wind would shift
and the air wasn't so bad, we'd walk west or south to
where there were cops and National Guardsmen sta-
tioned at every intersection. Tired, stiff-legged, and
bored from standing all day, they were always happy to
see her, grateful for a few precious moments with a
warm soft dog.

Too quickly after the attacks, the mayor began
advising people to return to normal. Go back to work,
went the counsel, back to routines—back to traffic
snarls and vicious horn-honking, fur pants and gossip
columns and stretch Lincoln Navigators almost a city
bus long. I quietly feared my own life might slip back
into itself as well. How could it not? There seemed only
one way to prevent it: Adopt George.

Five days after thousands of New Yorkers left for
work in the morning and never came home, Phil and
Peso and I returned to Union Square. A week earlier,

there had been a pro-parks rally in honor of the upcoming mayoral primary. Music and stump speeches rang out from a temporary bandshell at the south side of the park, garnering passing interest from people on their way to and from the greenmarket across the square. Seven days later, in a radically different reality, the park had become a massive shrine to the dead and missing. Dizzying altars of candles, flowers, photographs, and collages blanketed the square from end to end, and throngs of people—thousands of them—drifted among the memorials, sobbing.

It seemed impossible that this was the same park as the week before. Yet there on a little island on the southeast edge were the Mighty Mutts dogs and their apparently unflappable volunteers. A horrific sequence of events had made gruesome history, but of course for the dogs it was just another Saturday afternoon. There was George, tied to the fence beside the folding table that held the adoption forms and the donation jar, with his head resting in the lap of a volunteer. He still needed a home, same as ever. We left from the square that day with Peso and George, tugging on their leashes side by side. And from then on, nobody mistook us for normal.

Miraculously, Peso embraced her new brother. The first few days were hairy, as we tried to assuage Peso's confusion and jealousy while still making George feel at ease. Peso lunged at George every time he came back from a walk, though thankfully he never fought back. In a stroke of genius, Phil quickly taught her to regard George's crossing of the threshold as akin to the arrival of a new toy, so that she began to greet him with the same wiggling bouncy enthusiasm with which she greeted us. After only a week, they were falling in love, beginning each day by writhing together on their backs, licking and nibbling each other's ears, lips, and tongues (before proceeding on to less appealing areas). Was Peso trying to tell me something by her unexpected acceptance of George? The moral of this story, I remind myself, is that change is good, that even if we initially fear it we can adapt swiftly enough. (Therefore I must make the leap and leave New York.) But another possibility nags at me: Could the moral be that, with a little effort, we can grow to enjoy our surroundings, can even learn to love living side by side in small spaces? (Therefore I must resign myself to staying put.)

While I try to plot a responsible exit, I look after the dogs. Up in Vermont, they run wild in the fields; George bounds through the long grass, flashes of his long neck and shiny black-and-white coat visible as he leaps between cattails, like some zebragiraffe hybrid. Sweet, loyal Peso watches with admiration, though she tends to stay closer to home. Back in the city, George takes his seat at the window and barks. He expresses exactly what I feel. If I could get away with barking at all the people walking by, I would do it in an instant. "Why are you all here?" I imagine him asking. "Why do you put up with this place? Why don't you go live by a river, where you can run in the grass all day? That's where we're going!"

Sitting at my desk across the room, all day long I hear little kids' voices calling out from the street below in wonder, "Look at the doggie!" Of course, George's booming bark scares the hell out of some of them. But I forgive him. We'll be out of here soon enough.

AND THEY CALL IT CALL IT PUPPY LOVE

Elissa Schappell

Fang is my true-blue companion, you say. For richer for poorer, in sickness and in health, I can always and forever count on Fang to be true. That is until a milk truck rumbles by, or a rabbit darts out of the shrubbery, or God forbid a slobbery old tennis ball should materialize out of nowhere. . .

I ask you, which would you rather be thrown over for, a bosomy redhead or a slobbery old tennis ball?

So, he leaves me, the dog lover says*, he always comes back.*

Dogs are loyal, the dog lover says.

Loyal! Loyal, like a stalker boyfriend is loyal. Now, certainly people who abandon or mistreat their pets, or take embarrassing home movies of them repeatedly crashing headlong into a fence or falling off the back of a speedboat, deserve their own subsection of hell (a dark airless basement with only a washing machine and dryer going 24/7, no water, and a chipped plate scabbed with Alpo). I can't help but imagine that some of these folks who abandon Mr. Jinx had their reasons for moving the family out of town in a van under cover of darkness. I can only imagine the looks on their faces when who should come scratching on the screen door, plain tuckered out, paws raw as hamburger? Why it's old Mr. Jinx! He's traveled cross-country to bite the baby on the stomach, and pee on the new rug!

I am suspicious of these courageous canines who

walk from Philadelphia to San Diego in search of the family who left them behind. Someone is helping these dogs. Tell me those dogs aren't riding the rails like canine hoboes, or hopping on buses like Rosie Ruiz in the Boston Marathon.

He always comes back.

Dogs are the shape that a certain kind of girl believes the soul of a dead boyfriend—usually one killed in a motorcycle crash or a casualty of war—returns in. *Look how he bobs his head when he listens to the Velvet Underground, he loves cold Chinese food and hates spiders, and he rolls on his back whenever I kiss him on the mouth. I've been reading him John Berryman's Dream Songs . . .*

This gorgeous mutt snuggles between the covers, licks away her tears, and, if further proof were necessary, howls inconsolably whenever she brings a Johnny Nobody home and into her bed. *How could you,* he moans. *Don't do it,* he jumps on the bed and barks, until finally he finds himself locked in the kitchen.

Dogs are the big talkers of the animal kingdom. They're always shooting off their mouths in magical realism novels, spouting philosophical nonsense. And it is always dogs who goad deranged postal employees and night watchmen into getting into trouble. Nobody ever says, *Tabby told me to scalp those waitresses.*

Still, dog people would have you believe that dogs are better than you and me. They love and protect their masters no matter what. As if to prove how generous and pure of spirit, how goddamn stouthearted dogs are, you always see them in commercials with people who need allergy medicine, have weak bladders or heart problems. As their owners ride tandem bikes, fly kites, or run on the beach the dogs galumph alongside their masters grinning, *I love you even if you are incontinent. Go ahead, run and run, if you collapse I'll drag you to the nearest emergency room!*

Dogs are pushy. They insist you love them, they drop their head on your knee and raise their eyebrows, *awww* . . . no matter how many times you mutter *Shove off* and not so delicately knock them on the head with a teaspoon, back they come, trot, trot, to lick your sandaled arches.

Their need is so naked, it's embarrassing. *I want you to want me.* Dogs possess little mystery, they are the love addicts of the animal kingdom, predictable as masochists. *Though he pulled my tail, and sent me away, I returned again and again to his harem . . .*

For those couples ambivalent about having a baby, puppies, small and warm with ridiculously good-smelling bellies, are the next best things.

While the dog is perhaps the closest domestic animal to a baby, the closest animal indeed is a monkey. A deceptively cute-looking creature who will fling shit at you, tear up the house, and, if the neighbors complain, get you arrested.

Still, couples who fear they aren't ready to commit, those who aren't sure if their relationship can weather days of sleeplessness and the responsibility of coming home every night to clean up another being's vomit, adopt dogs.

The upside of children, and I am certainly not encouraging anyone to have a baby, is they don't actually consume shoes, as a rule they don't urinate on the neighbor's boxwoods, or leap onto barbecues and grab sirloin steaks between their teeth, or if they do, the child's owners may choose, like many dog owners, to dose their rowdy loved ones with Ritalin or Prozac.

Dogs will not take care of you in your golden years.

However—and here, I grant you, is where the loyalty attribute becomes a factor—a peevish child can grow up and write a tell-all book about your shadow life in Amish country, and your fondness for country line dancing naked while eating bologna. Forget the incessant air guitaring, your failure to recycle, and the blond merkin in your top drawer. Family squeals. Dogs don't.

Which isn't to say dogs don't engage in unseemly behavior too. In my experience, all too often dogs behave like drunken rich people; forgoing any pretext of personal space, they are apt to leap on you at any moment, stick their tongue in your ear, sniff you in a most unsavory fashion, and then leave you covered in mysterious hairs.

Although you shook their hand, nothing, nothing else in your behavior gave these animals any reason to think pawing you was on the menu.

Cats on the other hand are like the French. They gaze into your eyes, they purr, scratch you a little when your attention wanders, and then they are off to the windowsill staring into space, either deep in an existential crisis or dreaming of cheese.

I find it a bit curious how much some people love their dogs. *Love them.* The dog lover's only rival when it comes to the sheer number of bumper stickers one can slap on a car are the born-again Christians. If only there was a sticker to appeal to them both, something like, JESUS LOVES ME AND MY LHASA APSO, or DOG SPELLED BACKWARD IS GOD. Who am I kidding? I am sure they already exist.

Dog fanciers select their canine companions as though they were mail-order brides, and have them shipped across the sea at great expense, anticipating their arrival with sweaty palms. *I know Jenny is a dark beauty who likes herding sheep and the great outdoors, I've seen pictures of her mom, so if that is any indication, Wow. Other than that I am just relying on my gut. I can't wait to meet her.*

I cannot imagine that half of these dogs don't drop dead from the culture shock. Imagine dignified dogs bred for corralling wild mustangs; dogs whose bloodlines can be traced back to the Ming dynasty, where their foredogs stood sentry outside imperial palaces, now reduced to hunting squeaky hedgehog toys under the La-Z-Boy in the rumpus room, or guarding the door of an apartment filled with nothing but impossible Dutch furniture and Cy Twombly paintings.

It is bad enough that people insist on clothing their dogs. Yes, yes, I understand the merits of a simple cable-neck sweater, especially on a Chihuahua, and certainly no one should have to turn their eyes on one of those poor greyhounds shivering, even in sixty degrees, as though they've been peeled. Even the idiotic rain boots I can see, but a sequined torch singer ensemble? A cheerleading costume? A wedding dress?

Don't laugh. Sigourney Weaver threw a wedding for her dog (who wore a Vera Wang gown), allegedly because Weaver's daughter thought it indecent to breed the bride without benefit of marriage. Later, when the stud failed to show up to see his squirmy progeny—*Men are such dogs*—the girl was distraught on behalf of her pooch. Talk about living out your dreams through your children.

A cat would sooner tear every hair from your head than let you dude her up in a fancy dress and march her down an aisle. Cats are cool. Cats elope.

Dogs have owners, cats have staff.

I know what you are thinking: *You hate dogs.*

Aha, what about Seeing Eye dogs, you say! *You hate them too?*

Pardon me, I am expressing an unpopular opinion. I am not a barbarian. Seeing Eye dogs are exempt. They are not really dogs, as they don't act like dogs. I like Seeing Eye dogs because they ignore you. They have no time for you. They are focused on their job, and thus can't be bothered to get on their hind legs and attempt to *dance* with you.

Seeing Eye dogs are swell. Just swell. Really. There is a whole long line of Seeing Eye dogs lined up in front of me at the gates of heaven. Every one of them politely curbing themselves when necessary.

I *am* suspicious of these *heroic dogs* you see on television and read about in the papers. It seems every other day another mute librarian slips into a storm drain only to be rescued by a pack of selfless beagles. My guess is that she had half a ham sandwich in her pocket. Dogs are always saving people who probably would have been just fine, like the overeager lifeguard who races into the shallows to "save" pretty girls just so he can feel them up.

Though a dog will try to look modest as the mayor of the city slips a medal over his head for alerting the customers at Starbucks that the rest room was on fire, thus saving the lives of an entire gated community, they are so pleased with themselves, so smirky.

Dogs are just big show-offs. *Oh look at me, in my bandanna and sunglasses! Watch me run in a circle, watch me jump. I can jump high. Oooh, look at me! I can catch a Frisbee in my mouth!*

Yeah, well, so can I, but you don't see me hogging an entire hour on ESPN, do you?

If these dogs are so talented, and have so much time on their paws, why don't they do something worthwhile like turn a big wheel and create water energy for a small New England town?

Why don't they dig some ditches? Are these dogs too *good* for roadwork? Hmmm. Why not get them working on Route 95. Why can't all that lusty bouncy dog energy be harnessed for the good of us taxpayers? Mush, I say, mush.

Assembling a workforce of dogs is a great idea, but Americans would never go for it. Americans love their dogs like they love their guns and apple pie, and that is why I cannot be president of the United States: I will not get a dog. Saying you don't like dogs in this country is like saying you cut up the American flag for dust cloths. Saying dogs stink is like calling the Statue of Liberty a *ho*.

Harry S. Truman once said, "If you want a friend in Washington, get a dog." Truer words, it seems, were never spoken. Presidents from Washington to Bush have had dogs. Thomas Jefferson had a hummingbird, and John Quincy Adams kept silkworms along with a pet alligator, but a good 90 percent of the rest had dogs. Lots of dogs. Packs of dogs. Good dogs are like good soldiers: loyal, forthright, and ready for action. Traveling with a gang of dogs is akin to traveling with one's own army, and you can't have too many.

George Washington had fifteen hound dogs, among them Mopsey, Taster, Sweet Lips, and Lady Rover. Among his seven dogs, Herbert Hoover prized two police dogs, King Tut and Pat. Lyndon Johnson howled duets in the Oval Office with his adopted stray named Yuki, but was primarily a fancier of bea-gles. A photograph of Johnson hoisting his pets, Him and Her, by their ears incited the ire of animal rights activists. For presidents (and actors who want to bur-nish their Don't Hate Me Because I'm Rich, Beauti-ful, and Famous image—see Julia Roberts, et cetera), having a dog says *See, I'm just like you*. Richard Nixon's television address in which he cited his wife Pat's cloth coat and his spaniel Checkers as proof he was just folks no doubt rescued his vice presidential candidacy, paving the way for future high office. Real man-of-the-people president Jimmy Carter had his dog Grits. Ronald Reagan's fancy pooches, Rex, a cavalier King Charles spaniel, and Lucky, a Bouvier des Flandres, combined his flair for 1980s excess with his passion for lap dogs. Bill Clinton's devoted chocolate Labrador, the only one willing to walk to the plane with him after the Lewinsky scandal, was appropriately named Buddy. As in, *Hey buddy can you spare a pardon?*

When it seemed Clinton's life couldn't get much worse, Buddy was killed by a teenage driver. The loss of his dog brother seemed to devastate Clinton more than the Republicans stealing the presidency.

When George Senior was in charge, Millie the family spaniel channeled her story, *Millie's Book,* through First Mama Barbara Bush. Not surprisingly any bouts of ringworm, ticks, or fleas that Millie (or any other Bushes for that matter) might have suffered go without note, as does any mention of abuse of doggie uppers or Laxatone, by Millie (or any of the other Bushes for that matter). Likewise, Millie is mum on the matter of the birth of her puppies being induced to coincide with a visit by a national TV news crew. However, even without all these salacious tidbits, sales of *Millie's Book* somehow managed to handily outstrip sales of George Senior's autobiography. What does that say about our culture?

The current Bush in chief named his Scottish terriers Spot and Barney, no doubt after two characters in American culture that make him laugh. Spot from *See*

Spot Run, and Barney . . . Now is that Barney Fife or Barney Frank?

Barbara Bush herself resembles nothing so much as the gentle jowly bulldog who, though she appears harmless, delights in taking a chunk out of anyone, *it rhymes with witch,* who messes with her pups.

This sort of erratic behavior is typical of dogs. You can't trust them. Even a gentle-looking, lifesaving St. Bernard will, given half a chance and a snort of brandy, attempt to hump you into a coma.

Say you are a tiny bit frightened of dogs, and dog people will smirk . . . *and the dark too, right?*

Profess a fear from childhood—say, a dachshund bit off the bottom half of your best friend's face—and dog people will roll their eyes and scoff, *Oh, yes, well those little wiener dogs, they can't be trusted with small children.* Dog people will say this the way they might upon hearing of a mother who returns home and finds the crib empty, *Oh yes, well those crack-smoking baby nurses, they can't be trusted with small children.*

In the manner of parents of bullies, dog people refuse to acknowledge or take responsibility for the fact that their hairy drooling children have done wicked things. Secretly, you believe, they are proud of their alpha asshole children. *It's a dog-eat-nice-people world* seems to be their motto.

It is not unheard of for a dog owner, upon returning from hanging up your coat, to discover you in the breezeway shrieking and clasping the bloody stub that once was your arm, to see their sweet Petunia gnawing on your hand like a baseball mitt, and instead of smacking Petunia smartly on the snout, thus releasing your hand while there is still time to sew it back on, narrow their eyes at you and demand, *What happened here? What did you do to her? Well, you must have done something.*

Yes, yes you're right, you're right. I scratched my nose.

Yes, perhaps once it occurs to them that you might sue them, after all the loss of a hand is quite a substantial handicap, although no doubt there are dogs right now being trained as amanuenses, they will say, *Now, you bad doggie, you apologize. That's right give the nice lady her hand back.* Secretly though they are thinking, *God, what a complainer this gal is.* You can bet that as soon as the front door shuts behind you, the two of them are jumping on the sofa and rolling on the floor, licking each other's faces, howling with laughter at your expense.

A dog's affection and allegiance are repaid tenfold. So much so that I wonder, now somewhat uneasily, if the loyalty dog lovers feel for their dogs is stronger than the loyalty they feel toward their friends, say, those who aren't wild about dogs?

I suppose we'll see.

BODHISATTVAS

Chuck Palahniuk

"We flew down through Miami to Tegucigalpa," Michelle Keating says, "and this was after five days of terror. There's landmines. There's snakes. There's starving people. The mayor of Tegucigalpa was killed the week before in a helicopter accident."

Looking at pictures in a pile of photo albums, Keating says, "This was Hurricane Mitch. I'd never imagined I would go to a disaster like that."

In October 1998, Hurricane Mitch struck the Republic of Honduras with 180-mile-per-hour winds and days of heavy rain—twenty-five inches in a single day. Mountains collapsed. Rivers flooded. Some 9,071 people died in Central America; 5,657 in Honduras alone, where 8,058 people are still missing. One-point-four million were left homeless, and 70 percent of the country's crops were destroyed.

In the days after the storm, the capital city of Tegucigalpa was an open sewer, buried in mud and bodies. Malaria broke out. So did dengue fever. Rats carried leptospirosis, which causes liver and kidney failure and death. In this mining city, five thousand feet above sea level, one-third of all buildings were destroyed. The city's mayor died while surveying the damage in a helicopter. Looting was widespread.

In this country where 50 percent of the 6.5 million

people live below the United Nations poverty level and 30 percent are unemployed, Michelle Keating and her golden retriever, Yogi, came to help find the dead.

She looks at a photo of Yogi sitting in an American Airlines seat, eating an airline meal off the tray in front of him.

Talking about another search and rescue volunteer, she says, "Harry said, 'These people are hungry and they might want to eat your dog.' And I was driving home from a meeting with him, I was going, 'I don't want to die!'—but I knew I wanted to go."

She looks at pictures of the fire station in Honduras where they slept. Rescue dogs from Mexico had already arrived but weren't much help. A dam above the city had collapsed at two in the morning.

"A forty-foot wall of water had gone through and then receded, leaving just this deep, deep mud," Keating says. "Everywhere the water and mud had touched a dead body, there was the smell. That's what was confusing the Mexican dogs. They were hitting everywhere."

Looking at photos of the swollen, muddy Choluteca River, she says, "There was dengue fever. There was the germs. Everywhere you went, you could smell dead bodies there. And Yogi couldn't get away from it, and he wasn't wagging anymore at all.

They had a water shortage, but we'd wash everything down as much as we could."

In the pictures, people shovel the mud out of the streets in exchange for government food. The smell of the dead was "pungent," she says. "You could taste it."

She says, "Ten thousand were killed throughout the whole country, and a good percentage of them were right there in Tegucigalpa because they had the landslides, too. So there were the people drowned by the forty-foot wall of water coming through town. Then the soccer field caved in."

She shows photos of dim rooms, half filled with dirt and broken furniture. "The first day, we went to a Chinese restaurant where this family had died. The fire department would have to excavate, and what we were able to do is save a lot of time for them, and grief, because we'd pinpoint exactly where. In the Chinese restaurant we put Mentholatum under our noses and wore masks and a helmet with a light because it was dark. All the food, like crab, was spoiling and the sewers had overflowed, and it was knee-deep in mud. And there were all these dirty diapers. So Yogi and I go back into the kitchen, and I thought, 'Oh my gosh, what am I going to find?'"

In the photos, she's wearing a miner's hat with a light mounted on the front, and a surgical mask of gauze.

"There was all their clothes and personal effects embedded in the mud," she says. "People's entire lives."

They found the dead, crushed and twisted. "It turned out they were under a platform. There was a low platform that tables and chairs were on, and the water had forced them under there."

Michelle's sitting on the sofa in her living room, the photo albums on a table in front of her. Yogi sits on the floor at her side. Another golden retriever, Maggie, sits in a club chair across the room. Both dogs are five and a half years old. Maggie came from an animal shelter after they found her, sick and starving, apparently abandoned by a breeder after she'd produced so many litters she couldn't have more.

Yogi, she bought from a breeder when he was six months old and couldn't walk.

"It turned out that he has elbow dysplasia," she says, "and a couple of years ago I took him to a vet in Eugene who did surgery to allow him to walk. It reseated the joint. What had been happening was, this small joint—it was supposed to be a strut—but it was taking the weight so it was fragmenting, and it was very painful for him."

Looking at the dog in the club chair, she says, "Maggie's more the red, smaller kind. She's probably about seventy-five pounds. Yogi's the larger, blond, longhaired fellow. In the winter he's over ninety pounds. He's got the typical golden big butt."

Looking at older pictures, she says, "About eight years ago, I had a dog named Murphy. He was border collie/Australian shepherd mix, an incredible dog, and I thought, 'Here's a good way to work obedience with him and maybe meet some people.' I was working at Hewlett-Packard, in an office situation, so I needed a balance.

"The more I did it, the more intrigued I was by the cases. It started out as this dog-focused obedience thing and evolved into something that I really had more of a passion for."

In the photos of Honduras, Michelle and Yogi work with fellow volunteer Harry Oakes Junior and his dog, Valorie, a mix of border collie, schipperke, and kelpie. Oakes and Valorie helped search the ruins of the federal courthouse after the Oklahoma City bombing.

"Valorie, when she smells a dead body—or what she's looking for—she'll start barking," says Michelle. "She's very vocal. Yogi, he'll wag and get very excited but he barely says a word. If it's a deceased victim, he'll whine. His tail will go down and do the stress reaction."

She says, "Valorie will get hysterical and start crying. And she'll dig, if it's mud with someone underneath. Or if it's water, she'll jump in the water."

Looking at the photos of collapsed houses, she says, "When someone is either stressed or angry or anything, they let off epinephrine. And when violence or death happens it's just a more intense release of those smells. Plus whatever gases and fluids belonged to the body when it died. You can imagine in the wild why that would be so important to a pack. To an animal that means, 'Something has been killed here. One of my pack members has been killed here.' They get particularly upset over a human because we're part of their pack.

She says, "About 90 percent of the training to do search and rescue is the human recognizing what the dog's doing naturally. Being able to read Yogi when he's stressed.

"Obedience sets the tone that you're in charge. Then you hide toys from them; I still do that. And they love it. They have a race to see who can find it first. The next thing you do is have someone hold the dog while you run away and hide. You just keep doing more and more complex situations. They're looking on a track. If they haven't seen where you're going, they can smell."

Looking at a photo of a group of men, she says, "This is the Venezuelan fire brigade. We said we were the Pan-American rescue team."

About another photo, she says, "This is the one area we called the car graveyard."

About a vast, sliding hillside of mud, "This is the soccer field that collapsed."

Of another photo, inside a house filled with mud, she sayes, "Walking through this house that had been looted, there were handprints on the wall. All these mudprints where the looters had kept their balance."

In a wide band along all the walls are countless perfect handprints in brown mud.

In other photos are the rooms where Yogi found bodies buried under fallen walls, under mattresses.

One photo shows a neighborhood of houses tumbling down a steep cliff of mud. "This is up on the hill where all these houses had collapsed," she says. "They had hundreds of stories why people wouldn't leave: They didn't want looters to get their stuff; a woman with kids said her husband had gone to a bar and told her to stay here. Just awful, tragic stories." Another photo shows Valorie sleeping in the back of a pickup truck, dwarfed by a thick roll of dark, plastic bags.

Michelle says, "That's Valorie with the body bags, exhausted."

She talks about her first search. "It was up in Kelso, and it was a fellow whose wife had disappeared. There was word that she was fooling around with all types of different people who were coming up to the house. So we drive up to this immaculately manicured farm. There's horses and a pasture with a bull in it. The dogs did a huge death alert in the barn. Their tails go down and they pee. They swallow a lot. The natural part is the defecating, that and the peeing and the whining and the crying. It's making them nauseated, I think. Yogi pulls away. He doesn't want to go near it. Valorie goes toward it and she digs and barks more and more, and she gets frantic because she's trying to communicate something. 'It's right here!'

"These people's little boy, he was about four, said something to the grandmother about, 'Daddy put Mommy underwater,' and they whisked him away and nobody was able to be alone with him after that."

In another picture from Tegucigalpa, a long slab of concrete lies on its side in the middle of a riverbed.

"That was a bridge," Michelle says.

In all the pictures are scattered little packages of rancid lard, left everywhere by the water.

"The most profound search that I'll still get choked up about was this autistic child," she says. "The little guy was four years old, and they'd locked him in, but he'd found a way to unlock the door while his mom was ironing upstairs. He'd take all his clothes off, too, as soon as he got out the door. So all these people had volunteered to go look. And that's not optimal, because everytime one more person walks across the trail, they can track the scent somewhere else."

In these older photographs, Michelle is working with Rusty, another golden retriever. The photos show heavy woods around a slow, dark slough of stagnant water. "Within an hour of getting there, we got down to the slough. This is the primary spot because the little boy, he liked throwing a toy in repeatedly and pulling it out. It was just a little bank above the slough with roots and trees around it.

She says, "By then Rust was real distraught and really sad. That was the first place where the kid went in, so there was a certain kind of scent there. It wasn't as strong as when we followed the really slight current in the slough down to where it was getting stronger and stronger. That's when we called the divers in. There was a culvert between two parts of the slough."

Looking at the photos, she says, "What happened was the body had gotten wedged in this culvert, and it was under mud."

Petting Yogi, she says, "This is quite a large water area, and I'm going around, getting death alerts all around this huge marsh area. And I'm marking everywhere we get the hits. All that water that had touched the body had the smell of the death on it. Sometimes you can triangulate and determine where the body is by where the alerts are coming from.

"Putting a tag, and where the wind was coming from," she says. "What the temperature was. Who I was. What time it was. We put it all on a map. To figure out where the body had drifted to.

"Air scenting, in a case where you don't know exactly where the person started, there's still the scent in the air. There's a scent cone that goes like this"— she waves her hands in the air— "and you can get the dog to work a Z pattern. They might do it naturally. You want them to go toward the source of the scent."

Still petting Yogi, Michelle blinks, her eyes bright with tears. "I look up, and they're pulling him out of the culvert. That's the only victim I've ever seen because most of the time—like in Honduras—they come in and dig the victims out after we've left. But I went into deep shock the moment I saw him, and I had this profound urge to just hold him, this little guy.

"We got up to the house and did different interviews and then went into the house to cheer up the family—because the dogs are supposed to cheer up the family—and it was like walking through this aura, this energy . . . like an environmental condition . . . like being in a fog. We didn't process this like we should have," Michelle says. "I came back home and put Rusty with the other two dogs, to play, and I went off to work. I've always felt like that stuck with him too long because I didn't debrief him, and I don't think I knew how to process it. I don't think I understood what happened—as far as the deep shock—until I went to Honduras.

"You're supposed to let them go find a live person—and I did do that. You make sure, too, that you wash everything. Their jacket. My clothes. Everything that they have on. Wash everything in the car, everything that could've come in contact with the death scent. Just a little bit of that scent and they're depressed again."

She says, "Going back home, the scent pretty much permeated the car so it would've been good to clean that out as well."

Rusty and Murphy, Michelle's border collie/shepherd mix—like all the victims they found—are dead now. Murphy was put down when he was fourteen and a half years old, after suffering with back problems for three years. Rusty was put down after his kidneys failed.

Looking at photos of children, children hugging Yogi in picture after picture, Michelle talks about meeting a little girl in Tegucigalpa. Her legs running with staph infections, the girl was dipping water out of a puddle of sewage. Michelle put disinfecting tablets in the girl's water. A journalist rubbed antibiotic cream on the girl's legs.

"We had to walk most places because there was the mud, and everyone who saw Yogi would smile," she says. "And if we stopped somewhere, they'd just swarm around to touch him and say, 'Da me lo! Da me lo! Give him to me!' And he was just thrilled with it. He loved the attention. I know he understood how important the work was, and I'd tried to explain to him along the way, 'This is very important. You're doing good things for people.'"

In a picture of the collapsed soccer field, Michelle points out a crowd that stands at the far edge. "People would stand up here on the edge of the field and just watch us, and this one little boy said, 'Thank you,' in English."

She says, "Stuff like that would just destroy me. It was just too heartbreaking to have human contact like that."

She smiles over one picture. "We went to an orphanage to cheer up the dogs. A kid would run and hide, and then the dogs would find him."

Over the next picture, she says, "This is an island. We drove two hours over washboard roads and hairpin turns in the back of a dump truck to get there. This is the back of the dump truck, it's real dusty. We found three bodies."

She pets Yogi, saying, "I think it aged him. He's seen and smelled things most two-year-old pups won't have to go through."

In another photo album, Yogi sits with very thin, smiling men.

"I believe in bodhisattvas," Michelle says. "In Buddhism, there are beings that are enlightened and they come back to help others. I think Yogi's purpose in being with me is to help me be a better person and do things. For me, walking into Our House would've been difficult without him, but with him it was like home."

Talking about the AIDS hospice where she now takes Yogi, Michelle says, "I wanted something that was compelling and meaningful, and I kept hearing about Our House from people. At first I asked if they wanted someone to do Reiki, and they said no. Then I said I had this really neat dog, and they said come on over. And that was it. We just started going there every week."

Scratching Yogi's ears, Michelle says, "That's just part of his job. The comforting. That's what I mean by the bodhisattva—that he's more concerned with comforting and helping, almost even more than his own well-being."

Both dogs are asleep now on blue club chairs near a brick fireplace in this gray ranch house in the suburbs. The backyard is outside sliding glass patio doors, pocked with mud from the dogs running around.

She closes the album of Tegucigalpa, Honduras— the pictures of Hurricane Mitch—and puts it on a stack of albums.

She says, "It was just eight days. I think we did what we could."

YOU AND ME, BREATHING

Annie Bruno

When my dog, Seamus, was one and a half years old—just out of puppyhood and into his gangly ninety-pound adolescence—he had his first seizure. In the middle of the night my husband, Eric, and I heard a loud thumping against the wall, an adrenaline-producing sound, as if someone were breaking in with a hammer.

When we opened the bedroom door, I screamed then immediately wrapped my whole body as a cushion around Seamus, sure he'd been poisoned somehow and was going to die. But then, as if coming to from a violent dream, his legs stopped paddling and, panting hard, he got to his feet and tried to walk, wagging his tail to ward off his fear or maybe to tell us he was back, that he was okay.

We might not have even heard him if he hadn't been sleeping right outside our bedroom, if he hadn't been such a big dog. He was a greater Swiss mountain dog, square headed, mostly black but for the white socks on his four paws, a white swath that swept up his chest like a snowdrift, and a white blaze down his nose. He had tan cheeks, tan spots above his golden-brown eyes—a vestigial adaptation, my biologist husband explained, for looking awake while asleep at night to fool predators—and thin tan stripes that spiraled out from his tail and down his back legs like partly uncurled cinnamon rolls.

From puppyhood on, he looked right in your eyes every time you spoke to him. He was so beautiful that people stopped to stare. We would never have bought such an exquisite dog. We didn't know they existed, until a close friend of ours bought one and, after witnessing horrible, greed-induced breeding practices (Swissys, as they're known in dog circles, are still rare in this country, so breeders can charge up to sixteen hundred dollars for a puppy), became a breeder. She offered us Seamus as a gift because he was so special, because she couldn't bear to see him go to someone she didn't know. We loved him immediately, but even so said we needed a night to sleep on it. We'd been married less than a year, had just moved into our new little house. But after our friend took him back with her that first afternoon, we both felt we couldn't wait for him to come back. The house already seemed empty without him.

The morning after the seizure, we took Seamus to our veterinarian, who was cautiously optimistic. He didn't put Seamus on phenobarbitol right away, because many dogs will simply have one or two seizures and never have one again, or at least too infrequently to warrant medication. But in less than a week Seamus had a worse night, with multiple seizures this time, so we took him to the twenty-four-hour vet hospital in a nearby suburb of Washington, D.C. Seamus had stopped seizuring by the time we got him there, but the attendants rushed him to a back room and instructed us to go home, not to wait. They said they would keep Seamus under close observation. I'll never forget pulling up to our house the first time, both of us by habit looking in the empty front windows where Seamus would always be sitting, the top of his big head just grazing the underside of the tabletop.

That night in the hospital he continued to seizure, so they used anesthesia to break the cycle. When they reported this to us the next day along with a bill for nearly five hundred dollars, the veterinary assistant on duty had not been there during the night and so could only read the facts from a chart. We took Seamus home, grateful that he was alive, anxious to talk to Dr. Chuck to understand the facts. I felt scared he would seizure again, not sure I could stand it: the scared look in his eyes, his back legs giving way while his front legs stiffened straight out as he fell over, his whole body shaking as if caught in a bolt of lightning, mouth foaming. As with so many dreadful things, it's not so much the happening that wears you down as not knowing when it will happen, just that it will. The only calming thought we could share during our quiet ride home was that Seamus wasn't yet medicated. With medication, this surely wouldn't happen again.

That day Seamus began on a low dosage of

phenobarbitol, which held him steady for almost a week, but then he seizured again, not so badly this time, but it meant his dosage had to be increased. When Seamus seizured again a week later on the stronger dose, Dr. Chuck advised us to take him directly to a specialist clinic, telling us that he would call ahead and let them know we were coming. He said a veterinary neurologist would be able to start a stronger drug therapy, a combination of potassium bromide and phenobarbitol that was highly effective. He admitted he'd never seen a case that so quickly became this hard to control.

Seamus again had stopped seizuring by the time we got him to the specialist hospital. But he was unsteady, weaving as he walked, his pupils dilated. The assistant ushered the three of us directly into an examining room, where Eric and I lay down on the floor in an attempt to calm Seamus, who kept pacing and panting, stopping only to nervously kiss our faces.

When Dr. Knoeckel, the neurologist, arrived, his frame filled the entire doorway. Eric and I sat up, and Dr. Knoeckel knelt down on the floor with us while we finally got Seamus to stop pacing and sit. When we had accomplished this, Dr. Knoeckel took Seamus's face in his hands and looked intently into his eyes for a few moments, where there seemed to be a momentarily tense exchange. Then he scratched both of Seamus's ears and said, "I know. I know. You're a bright one," as if assuring Seamus that he'd heard his message loud and clear. I didn't know the message, but I knew we'd found the right person to help us save him.

During one of the many consultations I had with Dr. Knoeckel over the following months, he said, "The majority of dogs with epilepsy, like people with epilepsy, are very sensitive and intelligent. It seems a particularly cruel disease that way." He spoke of a concert pianist he knew who had to stop performing because he would often seizure on stage. Then he spoke briefly and painfully of his older sister who had died from the disease at age forty, after battling seizures her whole life.

He also said that medical science knew little more now about how the disease worked and how to treat it than it did a hundred years ago.

No one knew this fact better than my neighbor, Leticia, whose nine-year-old daughter Sophie had a case of epilepsy that was similarly difficult to control. Sophie didn't have grand mal seizures like Seamus's, hers were petit mal; she would stare off, lost to the world, trembling. She had several throughout the day at school, which made learning difficult. The side effects of the variety of medications they tried were distressing: sluggishness, inexplicable weight gain.

You'd never guess these trials. She was beautiful, bright, vivacious. When Seamus and I strolled past her house, she would run out to greet us, one time saying,

"Seamus if you kiss me any more I'm going to have to put on my swimsuit." When I told Leticia about Seamus's epilepsy, I'd found one person besides Eric who understood why we were doing all we could to fight the disease. When Leticia told Sophie that Seamus got the "flutters," she immediately threw her arms around his neck, saying, "Oh, I get the flutters, too," her musical voice a mixture of relief and consolation.

At each new stage between increased dosages or new drugs, the seizures that broke through were mostly violent. Sometimes a dramatic one would be followed by a mild one, which was usually a good sign that he would pull out of the cycle on his own. Our emergency trips to the hospital didn't end, though they got farther and farther apart. When he was hospitalized, sometimes he would only stay a day or two. A couple of times the seizures broke through even after anesthesia, and he had to stay longer. Those times the staff (all of whom I soon knew by name) stretched the rules and let me stay beyond visiting hours, let me lie with him in his holding pen, where he slept on blankets I brought from home. I would also bring toys and a chewbone, in case he was up to it, and cookies for the staff. The bills ranged from four hundred to a thousand dollars per stay. We didn't have that kind of money, but we tightened our budget, went into debt.

This financial strain was compounded by the fact

that I had to cut back at my job and go freelance, because we couldn't leave Seamus alone for fear of his seizuring to death. What's fatal about epilepsy, for animals and humans alike, is stasis: going into a seizure, or a series of seizures, and not coming out. The other reason was that, like the seizures, Seamus's medications gradually increased in number, strength, and frequency. I needed to be there to give him three times daily his doses of, at first, pheno and potassium bromide together, then the additional diazepam tablets. Along with each increase in dosage was a period of adjustment, a few days where he would suffer from aphasia in the rear legs, a wobbliness that was difficult to manage on our hardwood floors, so we covered them with a mishmash of rugs: expensive wool ones that we were long past caring about preserving, cheap ones from Home Depot.

When Seamus's epilepsy "broke through" his medication, causing him to seizure, I learned to fill a wide-nosed syringe with diazepam and insert it rectally, where the drug would be absorbed quickly enough to stop the cycle and keep him out of the hospital. I kept a record of the days or weeks between bouts, always hoping it was the last one, or that the next one would be less severe. Anything was better than the nights we rushed him to the hospital after six or seven seizures, sure he'd never stop.

After more than a year, Dr. Knoeckel said as a last

effort we should try Neurontin, a drug that had had some success in treating human epilepsy. Curiously, little was known about Neurontin's effects on the canine variety, and when I asked Dr. Knoeckel why that was, he said simply that most canine cases never advanced far enough to try it. So there was a small, added incentive for what we were all going through: to save not only Seamus but other dogs, too, who still seizured on the traditional treatments.

But there was a much, much bigger incentive than that. Over that year and several months there had been weeks, sometimes a month or more, when Seamus was living a normal life, going on walks, sitting next to me outside cafés in Georgetown on brisk fall days licking the leftover cappuccino foam in my cup, hiking with Eric and me through the snow, as robust and lively and joyous as the healthiest dog in the world. The work of making his life the best we could make it and riding out the ups and downs of his condition made us more and more a family. In fact, without even realizing it, we suddenly felt like we'd begun the family we'd wanted to create together, where we would give the kind of love and support that neither of us had in abundance from our own families.

To most people it seemed an extreme sacrifice. Dogs were not people, they either said or implied. But that only bound the three of us closer, made our family tighter. We didn't really need anyone to understand why. Besides, my reason was so simple. I loved him, and this disease didn't seem worthy of taking his life. I did what I would do for anyone I loved.

Seamus and I were always genuinely delighted to see each other, affectionate and kind to one another. I knew things he liked, and he knew things that I liked. When I worked freelance at home, he knew my hours, and at five o'clock on the nose, he would come into my study and rest his velvety muzzle on my keyboard and swivel his eyes up at me, reminding me it was time to move on to more pleasurable activities, like walking down to the river to watch the sunset. As long as he had enough of a dog's life, I told myself, healthy enough to enjoy long walks with lots of smelling and marking, to fetch sticks and bark at the parishioners getting out of their cars in the church parking lot on the other side of a bank of vines in the backyard, I could throw a few syringes in my fanny pack before Seamus and I set out on a walk: We would stick with it and battle.

Many times I questioned that reasoning, always checking to be sure I wasn't keeping this difficult trial for him going for the wrong reason: because I couldn't face his death. Eric and I considered our alternatives at every juncture, but always came back to the feeling that his life was still good enough, that age or some combination of drugs might extend those wonderful periods of health.

Seamus's care was largely mine to handle, as Eric had a demanding position at a wildlife conservation organization. He, too, was saving animals. So as the months wore on, it came down to a faith that having come that far, I would know when Seamus was ready to give up. When his adjustment to the medication went slowly or when I would visit him at the hospital, I would hold him and tell him that I didn't know why I was responsible to say when this disease was too much, when his life (which in nature would have been decided quite quickly) would be over, but that I was, and I was doing my very best.

Over time we started letting Seamus sleep on the bed. When he seizured, it was often in the night, and this way we could treat it right away and minimize the effects. The bed was pretty crowded. Seamus usually curled up between our feet, but sometimes he would wedge himself between us. His back was about the same length as mine, and several times I'd wake up to find he'd somehow stolen my pillow.

But when Eric traveled for work, which was fairly often, there was plenty of room. One February morning, three weeks shy of Seamus's third birthday, I was jostled awake by his body, which had lost him again, gone out of control. I threw off the blanket, scrambled to my knees, and tried to wrap my arms around him, trying to cushion his head as it shook its long, unrelenting *No*.

When the seizure was over, I cradled his jaws in my hands and tried to help stave off the next by staring into his eyes. As his forehead creased upward and his eyes widened in panic, I spoke loudly, "You're back and I'm right here. You're back. I'm right here."

As always he wanted to get up immediately and jump down off the bed, move about as if nothing had happened. I helped him down to the rug-covered floor. He was standing, barely. It took a while for his legs to move right. Weaving, he headed for the living room. I glanced at the clock. I didn't want to, but time was always our measure of hope, of health. The daily prayer: Maybe there won't be another one.

I followed him around the house, trying not to hover or look panicked, trying to make everything feel as normal as possible. I knew from experience that Seamus's anxiety was eased only by the regular routine of our day. I let him out into the yard and watched from the kitchen window while he wandered in the grass, sniffed the flagstones on the patio. I waited for him to bang the aluminum screen door with his nose, his loud, demanding knock that reminded me of the way, the moment he came to live with us, the house had become his.

He looked better, his eyes clearer. He took a long, loud drink of water, wolfed down half his food, then wandered into the living room. I listened hard to the silence until I heard him pick up a chewbone, even toss it around a little, before settling down for one of his tantric gnawing sessions.

Through the sound of the coffee grinder I suddenly heard that terrible rhythm through the kitchen wall. It was steady, flat—too rapid for hammering, too hard for knocks. I ran to the living room and pulled him away from the wall so that he wouldn't hurt his outsides, too. Even though he was still in it, lost to me, his legs galloping hard, I pulled him into my lap, using the kitchen towel I grabbed on the way to wipe his mouth, though it was being flung from side to side.

This one was longer, and his bladder went, as it had that morning, and I thought only that this strip of floor would be easier to clean than the mattress, which later I would soak with soapy water and prop up to dry.

When the seizure was over, Seamus popped up his head, as if he'd been underwater, and even though he was panting, his eyes smiled gratefully as he settled his head on my thigh. I smiled back, though being there with his body in my lap filled me equally with joy and grief.

For some reason, he wasn't so unsteady this time, and I could tell he didn't want to be steadied. He headed for the back door, to be outside again, and even though I wanted to stay close to him, touching him, I watched him from the window. Let him be a dog.

I continued to make coffee. Regular life was a comfort for me, too, though seizures had nearly become regular. Like everything in life, I'd come to know them and was no longer afraid.

I poured the water into the maker, glanced out the window to check on him. He was writhing on the ground near the fence, under the tangle of vines where the birds like to huddle and sing. I ran out the back door and took a short leap off the patio. I didn't know how long this one was exactly, but by the time I reached him it was already over. And as I helped him up, I thought how much gentler it was out in the garden where there were no walls or floors.

I knew I had to call the neurologist, but I wanted more time. The harder I pushed away the thought that my time with Seamus was coming to an end, the stronger the thought returned. It was like a strong wind and this time I could not get the door closed. I dialed the hospital. My voice only got out every other word. I couldn't get enough air. While I waited for Dr. Knoeckel to come to the phone, I stroked Seamus's back. It was hard to look into his eyes.

I told Dr. Knoeckel the number of seizures, their spacing and duration. He told me we could hold off, but if he had one more in the next hour, I should bring him in. I knew it was inevitable, but I was thankful for the time he gave us to be together, for the way he used *we*. It was probably just the pronoun doctors of all kinds use to soften the difficult things they have to say, but in this moment it gave me the much-needed sense that I wouldn't have to face this alone.

In the living room, I put on soft music, but Seamus slid back his ears and gave me a look that said he didn't want it, so I shut it off, lay with him on the rug. It felt like the safest place. He finally fell asleep, exhausted, his face pressed into the fleshy part of my upper arm. I smelled the fresh dirt from the garden, watched the wavering boughs of a young tree outside the window. All I wanted was to hold him forever like this, feeling his ribs rise and fall. All I want in the world is this, I told him. You and me, breathing.

I woke him after only a few minutes, because seizures mostly happened when he slept. His eyes fluttered closed, then opened wide, fearful. I eased his head back onto my arm, let him fall back to sleep.

I wasn't ready when he started to tremble, when his presence, again, evaporated. I panicked, calling him every name I've ever had for him, Seamus-puppy, Goofy, my big snoopy, combining the names, saying them over and over, as if it would make the seizure stop, rocking with his quaking body, until finally his eyes focused again. He was panting so hard. His tongue was violet.

Though I didn't want to leave him on the floor alone, I had to gather up his drugs in the kitchen in case he seizured in the car, and for his stay in the hospital, to save money on the bill. My throat swelled. Saliva filled my own mouth. I kept talking to him, trying to keep my voice smooth and soothing, as I threw all the burnt-orange vials of pills and the diazepam syringes into a paper bag from a gourmet grocery and wrote SEAMUS on the outside. I was desperate about not having written it more neatly. I was desperate.

I ran out to the driveway and opened the car door, set the bag in the front seat, and opened the back door, too. Seamus could walk to the car, though he wove quite a lot and I had to hold him up with a long towel I'd looped under his chest, just behind his front legs. We got his front legs in first, then I lifted in his back legs by the haunches and he lay down, exhausted, on the bed we'd made in the back of the SUV, the bigger-than-we-needed car we'd purchased to make it easier to take along our big dog everywhere we went.

Backing out of the driveway, I glanced back at the house while a car passed in the street and noticed that I'd accidentally left the front door open, wide open, and I thought: Let them take everything. The house will never be more empty.

Over the next three days I cleaned the house and went to the longest movies possible: *The English Patient*, Kenneth Branaugh's *Hamlet*. I didn't see anyone, except Seamus, who was groggy, and we mostly lay together on the floor of his holding pen, breathing. I burrowed my face in his silky fur and asked him to let me know if it was time. If there was a way he could tell me. I didn't see Dr. Knoeckel, as it was the weekend, but we spoke by phone to arrange a meeting on Monday. Seamus had to be anesthetized twice. I was getting ready to face his death, which I would have to choose. Death over life.

Eric was far away, in Nepal. I got a message through and he called me back. He could hear it in my voice, but the reality couldn't travel that far. He said he trusted me to make the decision. I thought about waiting not only so that Eric could be there but so I wouldn't have to go through it alone. But waiting wasn't the best thing for Seamus. And I sensed, rightly or wrongly, that Eric would be relieved not to live through that moment of death.

On Monday, as I drove to the hospital, I cried most of the way. I told myself I didn't have to decide until I got there, until I saw Seamus. In a wide, mostly empty blacktop parking lot in front of the hospital, on a piece of land in transition between Maryland's suburbs and its rolling picturesque countryside, I took deep breaths, thought about how the last gift of love I could give was strength and utter presence. Decisiveness.

I walked into the waiting room, as I had dozens of times—in the middle of the night, panicked, Seamus weaving or, worse, Eric and I carrying him. Far better were the times I was there to pick him up. I'd stand where I stood that day, unable to contain my smile, waiting for the moment I would see his big black head and blazing white chest round the corner, pulling the assistant along, as anxious to see me as I him.

While the receptionist finished with another person, I scanned the leashes-to-borrow hung on the wall, the toys for waiting children scattered on a small rug in the corner, and I hung on to the thought that it didn't have to be today. After a year and a half, why today?

The young assistant who led me back to the holding pens tried to speak brightly. She said Seamus was doing okay, told me how much they all loved him. She said the only thing was, he'd developed a minor respiratory infection overnight and was now on antibiotics, too. I knew then that it was too much. And when I knelt down and saw the slightest green mucus inside the edges of his big black nose, saw his tired eyes, his weakened body, I knew he was ready to go.

I sat on the floor stroking Seamus. I leaned forward to kiss his nose, stood, and met Dr. Knoeckel's eyes. I asked to speak with him privately, and he led me into one of the examining rooms near the front and closed the door. I sat in a chair and he leaned against the examining table. It might have even been the same room Eric and Seamus and I had waited in that first time, a year and a half ago, but this time I was alone.

He gave me the details of Seamus's condition, said the infection would heal in a day or so. I told him I thought it was time to stop trying. He asked if I was sure, and when I said yes, he told me simply and directly how we would proceed.

When he brought Seamus in, he unloosed the slip-knot lead so that he was without any collar, just his sleek black body. I looked into Seamus's eyes and asked him, in my mind, *Are you ready? Is it time?*

He was panting, looking directly into my eyes, too. His face was gentle, but I could feel his discomfort and didn't want him to struggle for another moment. I told him again and again that I loved him, that he was my puppy and always would be, that I'd loved caring for him, and finally, I told him how much I hoped there was a way he could come back to me, somehow, someday.

Dr. Knoeckel came in after half an hour, and he let me lie there and hold Seamus, just like I would do on our living room floor, while first he received a sedative and then something to stop his heart.

I felt him go.

Eric's colleague David called shortly after I got home. He wanted me to relay a message to Eric. I told him what had happened. He and his wife were good friends of ours. Seamus had, in fact, seizured at their house the previous Thanksgiving, but they had also joined us for a long snowy Christmas walk that year, where Seamus had torn around, high on the drug that snow seems to become for all dogs. David said he would come over immediately.

We went for a walk along the river, where we'd all walked that Christmas two months before. He was a quiet comfort. He spoke briefly of the loss of his father, who had died suddenly when he was a teenager, but nothing could change the enormity of walking there without my dog, without my husband: the two beings I loved more than anyone else in the world.

Almost two years later, Eric and I separated. There was no direct cause and effect from having gone through Seamus's illness and death and the death of our marriage. A marriage is far too complicated to fit into clichés like, *tragedy either brings you closer together or flings you apart*. What did feel similar, though, was choosing to end a life. Not just a way of life but a spirit. Marriage is a spirit as much as anything. A spirit that can grow and thrive and sometimes, like all spirits, fall ill and never recover.

Only now do I have enough perspective to know that those spirits never die. Love endures, no matter that physical connections cease to exist. I carry Seamus with me. I carry Eric with me. Love has many ways of being present.

From the moment you take a dog into your life, you understand that chances are you will outlive him. It's one of the many gifts dogs give: People must accept the inevitable loss, accept the terms of it, and grow in spirit because of it.

I'm still waiting for the right time for a dog. And as with the end of Seamus's life, I know that the right time will come. Until then, I drink in the pleasure of all the dogs I stop to pet and nuzzle on the sidewalks and in parks—the puppies, the old hobblers, all the lucky dogs with terribly rough starts rescued by kind people who make the space and give their hearts up to the greatness of their dogs.

When I think of Seamus, which is often, I still feel that mixture of joy and grief. I keep his collar on my desk. Sometimes I smell it or hold it to my cheek, the leather still soft even after five years, and I know without the slightest doubt that I would do it all again, in a heartbeat.

Contributors

Pearl Abraham is the author of the novels *The Romance Reader* (Riverhead Books, 1995) and *Giving Up America* (Riverhead Books, 1998), and the editor of the Dutch anthology *Een Sterke Vrouw: Jewish Heroines in Literature* (Meulenhoff, 2000). She teaches in the graduate writing program at Sarah Lawrence.

Annie Bruno lives in New York City. She's at work on a novel.

At the age of twelve, **T Cooper** rode the bus alone to see her first dog show at the Santa Monica Civic Auditorium. While she didn't become a dog fancier per se, she did develop a deep love for dogs. Besides raising little Murray Cooper, T is the author of the novel *Some of the Parts* (Akashic Books, September 2002). Her work—both fiction and non—has appeared in a variety of magazines, journals, and anthologies. T received an MFA in fiction writing from Columbia University. And for some time she doubled as T-Rok, a member of the all-star performance troupe the Backdoor Boys. For more info, visit www.t-cooper.com.

Nicholas Dawidoff is the author of *The Catcher Was a Spy: The Mysterious Life of Moe Berg*; *In The Country of Country: A Journey to the Roots of American Music*; and *The Fly Swatter: How My Grandfather Made His Way in the World*.

Ken Foster is the author of a collection of stories, *The Kind I'm Likely to Get*, which was a *New York Times* Notable Book. He is the recipient of fellowships from the New York Foundation for the Arts, Yaddo, and the Sewanee Writers Conference. His fiction and nonfiction have been published in *McSweeney's, Bomb, Flaunt, Salon, The New York Times Book Review, Village Voice*, and elsewhere. In addition to *Dog Culture*, he is also the editor of *The KGB Bar Reader*. He has taught at the New School and Florida State University, and is working on a novel.

Brent Hoff is a huge fan of Tom "Hot Tamale" Olifant but still feels really exhausted after that whole Doris Kearns Goodwin mess. He also believes this is the first time he has ever referred to himself in the third person, and he likes it.

Chris Offutt is the author of *Kentucky Straight*, *Out of the Woods*, *The Good Brother*, and *The Same River Twice*. His most recent book is *No Heroes*. His work has received many honors and is widely translated.

Chuck Palahniuk is the author of five novels: *Fight Club*, *Survivor*, *Invisible Monsters*, *Choke*, and *Lullaby*. His sixth novel, *Period Revival*, will be published in 2003. He lives in Portland, Oregon.

Hillary Rosner is a freelance journalist. Her work has appeared in *The New York Times, New York, Wired, Glamour, The Independent, Nerve*, and many other publications. Her last real job was as a senior editor at the *Village Voice*. She holds an MFA in creative writing from New York University and thinks someday she might try to write a novel. It will not take place in New York City.

Elissa Schappell is the author of the novel *Use Me*, which was runner-up for the PEN/Hemingway award, a *New York Times* Notable Book, a *Los Angeles Times* Best Book of the Year, and a Borders Original Voices selection. She is a cofounder of the literary magazine *Tin House,* where she is currently editor at large, and a contributing editor at *Vanity Fair* where she writes the "Hot Type" book column. She lives in Brooklyn with two Siamese cats and a hermit crab.

René Steinke is the author of the novel, *The Fires.* Her work also appears in the collections *With Love and Squalor* and *The Hot Spots: The Best Erotic Writing in Modern Fiction.* She is the editor of *The Literary Review* and teaches creative writing at Fairleigh Dickinson University. She lives in New York City.

Terese Svoboda's third book of prose, *Trailer Girl and Other Stories,* was published by Counterpoint Press in 2001. *Treason,* her fourth book of poetry, was published by Zoo Press in 2002. Her work has appeared in *The New Yorker, Atlantic, Paris Review, Harper's, Vogue,* and elsewhere.